Believing in Jesus

Believing in Jesus
Studies in the Gospel of John

Dennis R. Lindsay

Wipf & Stock
PUBLISHERS
Eugene, Oregon

BELIEVING IN JESUS
Studies in the Gospel of John

ISBN: 978-1-49824-809-9

Cataloging-in-Publication Data:

Lindsay, Dennis R.

      Believing in Jesus : studies in the Gospel of John /
Dennis R. Lindsay.

viii + 124 p.; 20 cm.

Includes bibliography

ISBN: 1-59752-655-X
1. Bible. N.T. John—Criticism, Interpretation, etc. 2. Bible.
N.T. John—Theology. 3. Bible. N.T. John—Homiletical Use.
I. Title.

BS2615.2 L5513 2006

Dedicated to the Members of the
Christliche Gemeinde Tübingen, e.V.
(1985–1992)

Contents

Introduction

*B*ELIEVING IN *Jesus* is one of the most important themes in the Gospel of John. Indeed, *Believing in Jesus* expresses, in a nutshell, the overarching missionary purpose of the Fourth Gospel. The most obvious indication of this appears in John 20:31, where the evangelist explicitly states that "these things are written *so that you may come to believe* that Jesus is the Messiah, the Son of God."[1] But this verse is merely a summary statement at the end of the Gospel. It highlights the missionary theme and purpose present from the very outset of the Gospel.

The Gospel's Prologue sets forth the missionary agenda of a testimony that draws people to believe in Jesus (see John 1:7, 12). The 'signs,' which are recorded throughout the Gospel, always appear in connection with believing in Jesus. Often, as with Jesus' very first sign, the changing of water into wine at the wedding feast in Cana, it was the very disciples of Jesus who believed in him (see John 3:11). Thus, these first disciples are typical examples of people who believe in Jesus and they become models for subsequent disciples of Christ in the generations to follow. This is the point that Jesus makes in his post-resurrection

---

[1] Italics mine. All scripture quotations are taken from the *New Revised Standard Version*, unless otherwise noted.

1

encounter with the doubting disciple, Thomas, in John 20:26-29.

Not only are the miraculous signs occasions in the Fourth Gospel for believing in Jesus, but also situations of controversy and hostile confrontation—for example, the cleansing of the temple in John 2:22-23; or the controversy over 'bread from heaven' in John 6:60-65, 69. Also, many of the major discourses of the Gospel are structured around the ultimate goal and response of people believing in Jesus–for example, the Nicodemus discourse in John 3; the account of the woman at the well in John 4; or the farewell discourse from John 14–17. The entire Gospel of John is structured around the crucial issue of believing in Jesus: "Those who believe in him are not condemned; but those who do not believe are condemned already, because they have not believed in the name of the only Son of God" (John 3:18).

Quite apart from the explicit statements of missionary purpose, however, the sheer frequency with which John the Evangelist employs the word 'believe' clearly indicates the importance of this theme. Forms of the Greek word *pisteuein* ('believe') appear over a hundred times in John. There is no New Testament author, including Paul, who makes more frequent use of this verb. The occurrences of the word 'believe' in John's Gospel account for well over one third of the occurrences in the entire New Testament. Believing in Jesus is truly a theme that is close to the Evangelist's heart.

But what does it mean to believe in Jesus? Is faith, in John's vocabulary, simply a matter of offering intellectual assent to a formula of facts relating to the person of Jesus Christ? Or is it rather a matter of encounter, challenge and commitment to this person Jesus? Or does faith, perhaps, involve a combination of all these things? Extremely significant for the author of the Fourth Gospel is the fact that *believing* is a verb rather than a noun. As a matter of fact, John never uses the noun *faith* (*pistis* in the Greek) in the entire Gospel. This is remarkable, given the fact that the verb *believe* (*pisteuein*) occurs more frequently here than anywhere else in the New Testament!

Believing is something very concrete for John, rather than an abstract concept. *Believing* is something in which Christ's disciples are actively engaged, rather than a passive state of mind or heart or emotion. *Believing in Jesus* is, in fact, modeled in the lives of men and women, who, through their encounter with Jesus Christ, become engaged with God in a new and vibrant way. In this engagement with God, there is nothing theoretical which does not have its corollary in the day-to-day life of the believer; there is nothing abstract which lacks its referent in praxis. *Believing in Jesus* is, for John, a *verb*!

The following studies in John's Gospel are offered in order to highlight this theme of *Believing in* Jesus. The individual studies were originally written as sermons and delivered for the *Christliche Gemeinde* (Christian Church) in Tübingen, Germany between 1987 and 1992. I owe a great deal to the members of that congregation for insights about what it means for Christians today to *believe in Jesus*. These studies do not exhaust the topic of what is involved in *believing in Jesus*, any more than the Fourth Gospel itself exhausts this theme. They are merely offered as examples, models, and patterns. For *Believing in Jesus* must be a present and ongoing engagement with God in the lives of Christian women and men.

This latter observation is one that I cannot emphasize enough. Believing in Jesus takes us to new destinations—sometimes places where we might never have imagined ourselves going. This has become very clear to me through this process of editing these sermons that were particularly meaningful to me—and to the flock under my pastoral care—some two decades ago. I find that my theology has shifted and many of my earlier opinions have softened. Colleagues, students, and friends who know me now might be surprised by some of my earlier ideas present here. This, perhaps, points towards the most important facet of believing in Jesus; that is, believing in Jesus does not permit the *status quo*. Believing in Jesus is less a matter of defining orthodoxy and more a matter of engaging daily with Christ and growing in discipleship. It is in this spirit that I offer these studies. Understanding more of what it meant for those first followers of Jesus to believe in him should be an aid and encouragement to modern-day disciples as they live out the practicalities of their faith and as they strive to share their faith with other people.

1

Look . . . The Lamb of God!
John 1:29-34

JOHN THE Baptist was the harbinger of a new beginning for the people of God. His message was concerned with a new era for the Church of God—a time when God would be active amongst His people in a refreshing, new way. "The Kingdom of God is at hand!" proclaimed John. "Prepare the way of the Lord! Make a good highway for His arrival! Raise the valleys! Level out the mountains and hills! Straighten out the curves! Get rid of the barriers! Repent! Get your life turned around! Be baptized so that your sins may be forgiven! Standing amongst you already is someone you do not yet recognize. He will baptize you with the Holy Spirit and with fire!"

With these and many other words of exhortation, John the Baptist was signaling a new beginning for the people of God. John was setting a new standard. From now on things would be different. "Even now the axe is lying at the root of the trees; every tree therefore that does not bear good fruit is cut down and thrown into the fire" (Matthew 3:10). These are words of revolution and radical

5

change. John left no doubt in the minds of his listeners that the time for a new beginning had come.

Indeed, the people of John's time were ready for a fresh start. They were ripe for the harvest of God's coming kingdom. Multitudes of God's people flocked to John in the desert. The crowds came not only from the area around the Jordan where John was baptizing; they also came from Jerusalem and from the whole region of Judea. The people who came to hear John represented virtually every religious, social, political and economic class from among God's people. There were peasants and artisans, academics and teachers of the law, soldiers, tax collectors, prostitutes, Pharisees and Sadducees. Many were fed up with life outside of God's kingdom. They were thirsty for justice, both in their personal lives and in their broader surroundings. They were hungry for a fresh start. They were ready for a radical reversal from the lives they knew.

Thus the people came *en masse* out into the wilderness to hear John preach about a new beginning. They confessed their sins. They were baptized in the Jordan River. They were filled with great anticipation and great expectation, setting their hope on a fresh start for their own lives and on a new beginning for the Church of God, of which they were naturally a part.

No sooner had the words of a new beginning come out of John's mouth, however, but there arose all sorts of difficulties. There was a great deal of confusion and even controversy over the meaning and exact nature of this new, fresh start for God's people. What precisely was the starting point? Likewise, what was the goal, the 'finish line' towards which this new beginning was directed? Was this new beginning to be understood in political, economic or social terms? Did John's message indicate a new beginning only for individual men and women who came to him, or was this something that concerned the whole people of God?

Further, there was much speculation about John the Baptist's own role in this new beginning. Who *was* John, after all? Was he the Messiah, God's Anointed One? Was he Elijah, the prophet of old who was taken up into heaven in a fiery chariot and now returned to earth? Perhaps he was that Prophet whom Moses had promised that the Lord would raise up from among his people? Certainly, many were convinced that John was the central figure in this new beginning for God's people. Surely he was the one on whom all eyes must focus.

But this was not to be the case. All of this was a misunderstanding on the part of the people who were going out to John. The new beginning for God's people was not necessarily the kind of beginning that they envisioned for themselves. John himself refused to allow the people to misconceive his own role in God's unfolding plan. John was not the central figure. He was simply the 'wilderness voice' in Isaiah's prophecy; he was the one crying out to prepare the way for the coming of the Lord's own special agent. John was the herald of one coming after him; indeed he was the herald of one who already stood in their midst. Pointing to Jesus John declared: "Here is the Lamb of God who takes away the sin of the world!" (John 1:29).

The clear indication of John's testimony is that Jesus is both the starting point and the goal of the new beginning for the people of God. The sacrificial Lamb of God defines the terms and sets the parameters of this fresh start, which is the kingdom of God. John is simply the herald.

With this prophetic word about the Lamb of God, it becomes apparent that the new beginning, which God holds out before us, is much different in nature from the radical reversal that many people imagine and desire. The goal of this new beginning has nothing to do with military victory over political enemies. It does not indicate a fresh start in terms of material goods or financial security. The primary impact of this new beginning is not even understood in terms of a society where human rights and equal rights are securely pinned down for all to enjoy. The metaphor of the lamb, which John uses to describe Jesus, does not suggest role of a politician or scientist or philanthropist. Rather, it conjures up the idea of vulnerability and sacrifice.

The new beginning announced by John is one that specifically involves the forgiveness of sin—the sins of the world! The starting point of this new pathway is fixed unmistakably in the person of Jesus Christ. This is what John the Baptist was indicating when he said:

> I saw the Spirit descending from heaven like a dove, and it remained on him. I myself did not know him; but the one who sent me to baptize with water said to me, "He on whom you see the Spirit descend and remain is the one who baptizes with the Holy Spirit." And I myself have seen and have testified that this is the Son of God. (John 1:32-34)

Believing in Jesus Christ, the Son of God, is the starting point of the new beginning that John holds out to the people of God. This is true not only for people who are already familiar with God, but this is the starting point for all people everywhere who are yearning for a meaningful fresh start in life.

Indeed, there are many people and many people groups throughout the world today who are looking for the possibility of a new beginning. The first time I delivered this particular study on John 1:29-34 was on 14th

January 1990 at the Christliche Gemeinde (Christian Church) in Tübingen, Germany. At that time East Germany and West Germany were still divided by walls of concrete and barbed wire patrolled on the East Side by armed guards with orders to shoot to kill. Yet political and economic refugees from East Germany and other parts of Eastern Europe were finding channels of passage into the sanctuary of the West and were literally flooding in by the thousands and tens of thousands. These refugees came to the West filled with visions of hope for a fresh start and a new life. In more recent years we have seen the same yearning looks on the war-weary faces of women and men and children in various parts of Europe and in every other part of the world where people are oppressed and afflicted in one way or another. The world is full of refugees who have had all they can take of the strife and problems of their homelands and native villages. They are hungry and thirsty for a fresh start for themselves and their families.

In the midst of a world oppressed by unrest, the Church of Jesus Christ is a sanctuary for refugees. The Church today shares with John the Baptist the proclamation of a new beginning, of a fresh start for the people of the world. Oppression occurs in myriad forms and no human society is exempt. Dissatisfaction with the status quo of day-to-day life is a universal human experience. The Church is never out of earshot from people who have made mistakes in their own lives, or from people who have suffered severe disappointment, or from people who have stumbled into insurmountable difficulties over which they no longer have any control. The Church is never far away from people who are suffering financial, spiritual, relational or physical difficulties, and who can find no possible way out. If only there were a chance for a fresh start!

But there is indeed an opportunity for a fresh start and for a new beginning. The Church of Jesus Christ is and remains the herald of this good news, once proclaimed by John the Baptist. The Church bears witness to Christ, just as John did. Those who are in Christ have personal experience of this new beginning in their own lives. Men and women who believe in Jesus are witnesses and messengers of the good news that God desires to create a fresh start for people. The Kingdom of God is at hand, and its doors are open to all people in all places.

We must, however, be perfectly clear in this one matter, just as John the Baptist was clear in his preaching. The starting point, the pathway and the goal of this new beginning are completely circumscribed and defined by Jesus Christ. The decisive figure that introduces this fresh start is the figure of a sacrificial lamb. The divine act, which creates the possibility for the new beginning, is God's act of forgiving sins. The starting point for women and men is the way of repentance and trust. Therefore, the Church who remains true to its calling as God's herald of a fresh start for the people of the world will faithfully bear witness to Jesus Christ. Our message of hope to the world today is the same as the message of John the Baptist: "Look! Here is the Lamb of God who takes away the sin of the world!"

2

Surprised by Jesus
John 2:1-11

G OD IS full of surprises! God takes delight in surprising his children who put their trust in him. God surprises us in ways that we could never have imagined and with provisions that we could never have thought to ask for in prayer. In particular, Jesus is full of surprises. How many times do we find Jesus in the gospel accounts doing something or saying something that catches his audience—even his disciples—completely off-guard? Particularly for people who are willing to 'stick their necks out' for Jesus, he seems to take delight in catching them off guard with some new and wonderful surprise.

We do not know who put Jesus' name on the invitation list for the wedding in Cana of Galilee. Perhaps it was some member of the bride's family, or the groom's. The village of Cana was only about ten miles from Nazareth where Jesus grew up, so that it is very likely that Jesus himself was related to the bride or the groom or that he was a close friend of the family. From the narrative in John's gospel Jesus' mother appears to have had some influence with the caterers at the wedding feast. In any case, we can be certain that everyone at the wedding feast in Cana had to be very pleased that Jesus was there. His 'little surprise' on this occasion saved the day!

As a matter of record, wedding ceremonies and celebrations always tend to be full of their own 'little surprises,' just by the very nature of this kind of event. Whenever there are so many people from different families, different backgrounds and different social settings who come together for a common occasion to celebrate the joining of a woman and a man in holy matrimony, there are bound to be surprises on the day. Often what we find in this situation is a recipe for surprise.

Moreover, not all of the surprises that take place at wedding celebrations are pleasant ones. I would venture to guess that there is not a wedding celebration on record where absolutely everything went according to plan and absolutely nothing went wrong. No matter how much preparation has gone into the event; no matter how meticulously the plans are made; no matter how much care is given to the most minute of details in order to assure that everything goes well; no matter how many prayers are offered up by the bride and her mother—in spite of all this, something will always go wrong! Perhaps at the very last minute the bride discovers a big tear in the wedding dress. Maybe the groom and other members of the wedding party are held up in a traffic jam and cannot arrive on time. The photographer is there with all the proper equipment, but has forgotten to bring film for the camera; or the five-tiered wedding cake more resembles the tower of Pisa—with the worst of results! It may not be a major glitch, but I would wager that every married couple who ever lived could tell a story about a 'little surprise' which occurred at their wedding.

At the wedding in Cana of Galilee they ran out of wine. Oh, the shame of it all! Oh, what a tragedy! What a disaster! How embarrassing for the family! *A wedding feast without wine!* What an unfortunate and unhappy surprise this was! So it was that Jesus' mother came to him and began to tell of the despair: "Whatever will we do? They have run out of wine! *It's the end of the world!*"

It was not, however, the end of the world, simply because a problem came up at a wedding feast in Cana. As a matter of fact, the world kept turning and would continue to do so. Those who were most affected, most disappointed, most embarrassed by this unfortunate turn of events would continue to live. One day soon the crisis would not seem so serious anymore. Time would bring about a new perspective; and someday the bride and groom would probably be able to look back on the event and laugh about how they ran out of wine at their wedding feast!

Life goes on in spite of life's unhappy surprises. If the bride discovers a big tear in the wedding dress, there is likely to be someone who can quickly mend it so that the 'show can go on' without major interruption. If the groom gets stuck in traffic, he will still arrive *sometime*. If the photographer forgets the film, there are always dozens of other people standing around with cameras and taking photographs. Likewise, when the wine supply runs out, it does not mean the end of the world. It is only the end of the *wine*!

I can imagine Jesus' lips curling into a smile when he commanded the servants to bring in the *water* jugs, and to fill them with *water*—all the way up to the brim! One hundred and eighty gallons of *water*! That ought to be enough fluid for the guests to wash down all that dry

wedding cake! They have run out of wine? Let them drink
. . . *Perrier!* Propose a toast with *H²0!*

Jesus then told the servants to draw some out of the
jugs and take it to the master of the banquet. The servants
obeyed. The master of the banquet tasted the water; but it
was not *water*—it had become *wine!* What a wonderful,
happy surprise this was: Water turned into wine!

I am reminded of a story that I first heard as a child
when a visiting preacher spoke at my home church. The
story was about an old, retired minister who was not terribly conscientious about practicing what he had preached
earlier in his life. As a matter of fact, he used to go every
Saturday evening to the local watering hole and carry on
drinking like a fish. One Saturday night after his drinking
binge he was on his way home—*driving,* of course—and
having a rather difficult time keeping the car on one side of
the road. Fortunately, a police officer was on duty, spotted
the old preacher and safely pulled him over. As the officer
stepped up to the old man's car, he spied a rather suspi-
cious looking bottle lying on the seat and questioned him
about the contents of the bottle. "Why, it's just *water,* officer", the man replied. Unconvinced, the officer grabbed
the bottle and took a big whiff, which just about knocked
him over. "That's not water," exclaimed the police officer.
"That's pure wine!" Immediately the old preacher's face
lit up like daylight, and he blurted out: "What a surprise!
Praise the Lord! *He done it again!*"

The fact that water was turned into wine is indeed
a big surprise in this story in John's gospel. People today
often get sidetracked at this point, trying to sort out exactly how Jesus pulled this off. What kind of trick was
that? Was it some kind of magic? Of course, we know that
John presents it as a miracle. Even more, in the context of
John's gospel, this event is portrayed as a *sign*; it is a sign of

Jesus' power and glory. Here was a situation where something had gone terribly wrong. It was a situation where we would have expected that this wedding celebration would have to go on without any wine to enjoy, or perhaps when we would expect that the celebration and feast might soon be over. But in this very moment Jesus Christ *surprises* us. He performs a miracle, a sign. He changes water into wine.

Water turned into wine is not the only surprise that we encounter in this story. There is an even more important surprise. It is the surprise that the master of the banquet experiences. His surprise in this story was of a completely different nature. When he tasted the sample of the water-turned-into-wine he had no idea that a miracle had been performed. He had not the slightest inkling that water had been turned into wine. He did not even know where this wine had come from. But he was indeed *surprised* when he tasted it. He called the bridegroom over and said to him: "Everyone else brings out the choice wine first; then when the guests have had plenty to drink and their taste buds are no longer so discriminating, they bring out the cheap stuff. *But you have saved the best wine until last!*"

This is the *main surprise* of the story. The wedding feast was, in fact, about over. The people had already been there feasting and celebrating for a long time, with plenty to eat and plenty to drink. They had been there long enough to exhaust the wine supply that had been catered. At this point in the celebration they could not have expected that the wine on offer would have been of the best vintage and quality. Indeed, they might well have expected that the wine supply would run dry soon, that the feast would be over and that it would be time for everyone to retire to their own homes. But it was precisely in this moment—when it looked like the celebration was winding down—that the very best wine was brought forward. What is more, *there were 180 gallons of it!* This was the enormous surprise!

It may be puzzling to many Christians (especially to those who have a strong aversion to alcohol) just how this miracle displays the glory of Jesus, as John tells us that it does. I would suggest that the answer to this puzzle is particularly apparent in the context of this latter surprise. That is, at the end of the day, God's very best gift is found in Jesus Christ and in him alone. The very best that there is in life is saved up for the last. It is God's big surprise, which we can only experience through Jesus Christ.

Of course, we are talking now about much more than water and wine and weddings. The fact that God's best is stored up until the last, only to be experienced through Jesus Christ, is a recurring theme throughout John's gospel. The realization of this revelation is almost always connected with a surprise. John 1:17 reminds us, for example, that the law was given through Moses. The law was a good thing; it was a prized possession of Abraham's descendants for centuries. But in Jesus Christ, God's *complete* character, God's grace and truth, confront us in physical form. God saves the best and biggest surprise until last!

Likewise, the woman at the well in John chapter 3 had enjoyed the good water from Jacob's well all her life. It was a wonderful, refreshing, life-giving gift of God to her and her people for centuries and centuries. But in Jesus Christ she found a surprising gift of God which was far greater than anything she could have imagined or asked for simply from her experience of Jacob's well.

Certainly the greatest of all the surprises which John's Gospel records was the surprise which the disciples experienced three days after Jesus had died on a Roman cross. Yes, they believed already in a resurrection from the dead. In fact, they probably believed in much the same way that we today tend to believe in the resurrection; that is, in very abstract terms and uncertain images. (None of us, after all, has actually had any concrete, empirical experience of resurrection!) But when the Risen Lord Jesus confronted the disciples on Easter Sunday and in the days and weeks to follow, they were utterly amazed. There was no way that their feeble minds and limited imaginations could ever have conceived of the glorious reality, the overwhelming *surprise*, which confronted them in the person of the Risen Lord!

It is in this light that we need to consider this miracle, this *sign*, which Jesus performed in Cana at the wedding feast. What Jesus did here is of much greater importance than simply rescuing a wedding feast from potential embarrassment. Jesus was not just saving a wedding; he was saving *people*. At this feast in Cana of Galilee Jesus gave a sign. It was a sign that clearly displayed who he was. The disciples recognized through this sign Jesus' divine glory. As a result of this, they *believed in Jesus*! And this is, after all, what it means to be saved!

These disciples were people who had already experienced the goodness of God in many, bountiful ways for many, many years. They possessed the Law of Moses. They had a national identity. They were heirs of a glorious hope for the future and of the wonderful promises of God. They had experienced so many good things from God's hand that they could scarcely have hoped for anything more, for anything *better*. But precisely in this moment, when they felt they had experienced the best of the blessings, and when it may have looked as though the blessings would soon be running dry—in this moment they encountered God's biggest surprise of all through Jesus

Christ. It was more than they could ever have imagined or hoped for.

Our world today is full of people who have experienced many good gifts from the hand of God—health, gainful employment, success, security, abundance of food, etc. This is true for the 'unrighteous' as well as the 'righteous', for God allows the sun to shine on the bad as well as the good and God sends life-giving rain upon all people, whether they honor God or not. We *Christians* have received wonderful gifts from God's hand. Sometimes, when things are going well, we cannot imagine how it could ever get better. Sometimes, when the going gets tough, it seems as though the blessings may be running dry and that we have already experienced the best that God has to offer.

But a *big surprise* awaits those who come to God by believing in Jesus! At the end of the day—at the end of every day—the very best that God has to offer is ours in Jesus Christ. God is full of surprises. Jesus takes delight in surprising his disciples who put their trust in him. He surprises us in ways that we could never imagine and in ways that we could never think to ask for in prayer!

3

A Strange Picture of Jesus
John 2:13-22

IN THIS modern age, who could possibly believe in the kind of Jesus presented in John's account of the cleansing of the temple? The Jesus described in this story is *different* from the Jesus which most people today expect. It is not the picture of Jesus to which we have become accustomed. The Jesus whom we encounter here is nothing at all like a "holy infant, so tender and mild" that we find "sleeping in heavenly peace" in our re-created nativity scenes at Christmas time. This is not the polite, well-mannered twelve-year-old who sat in the temple discussing the word of God with the elders and teachers of the Law. The Jesus of this story bears no likeness whatsoever to the soft, fragile, almost passive image of some ethereal 'God-man' portrayed in so many idealized paintings of the nineteenth century.

Where are the normal 'Jesus-characteristics' that we have grown accustomed to expect? Where is the love, the peace, the meekness and humility, the servanthood and self-sacrifice, the mercy and grace? Where is Jesus' openness to discussion and dialogue with his antagonists? Where is his patience and passive behavior? Where is the diligent search for a peaceful solution to problems? Where is the *Jesus* in whom people today want to believe?

What we see instead is a Jesus who becomes enraged over a sad and sinful situation that he finds in the Temple. It is a Jesus who burns with righteous indignation because unholy people have misused and abused the house of God. This is a Jesus who, in his anger, turns to radical (we might even say *violent*) action in order to restore the proper order in the Temple courts.

The Jesus in this story does not call a meeting of the church board in order to discuss the various possibilities of restoring order and dignity to the Temple as a house of God, after it had been turned into a market hall. There is no process of dialogue and discussion. On the contrary, Jesus pieced together a whip out of strips and bits of leather, which he readily gathered from the floor of the temple area. Then he employed this whip to drive all the cattle out of the temple courts with a display of force and violence.

If we had been there on that day, we would surely have heard the loud crack of the whip as it came down on the backs of sheep and cattle. We would have heard the bleating and the bellowing of those animals as they were being driven out of the temple. We would have felt the shock waves through the stone pavement as the tables of the moneychangers were violently overturned and crashed to the floor. We would have heard the distinctive sound of coins falling to on the pavement and rolling and scattering in every direction.

"Take these things out of here!" Jesus railed at the merchants. *"Stop making my Father's house a marketplace!"* (John 2:16).

I dare say that if Jesus were to appear today and to take this kind of action in a so-called 'house of God', he would find himself very quickly in a heap of trouble. There would be an emergency meeting of the elders, and they would be quick to censure this kind of outburst. The local, national and international church councils would do their best to distance themselves from this religious fanatic, because of the unpopular press coverage he attracted. Denominational officers, in their embarrassment, would look for some possibility, some loophole, to rescind the ordination of this person and make sure that he did not continue in the ministry. Jesus surely would not have found it very easy in dealing with the religious leaders of today, if he were to try something like this again!

Indeed, this adverse reaction of the leading religious leaders was precisely what Jesus encountered on the day of the event. Jesus had stirred up a hornets' nest amongst the leaders in Jerusalem in his own day with this so-called cleansing of the Temple. "Who allowed you to do this?" they protested to Jesus. "What sign can you show us that you have this authority?"

"Destroy this temple," Jesus replied, "and in three days I will raise it up."

This further word of Jesus was the last straw for the religious leaders in Jerusalem. In their view, Jesus had already *desecrated* the Temple with his display of violence. But now he was speaking of the *destruction* of the temple. This was nothing less than blasphemy against the holy place of the Jews; and blasphemy against the temple was tantamount to blasphemy against God! It really comes as no surprise that later on, in the trial of Jesus before the High Priest, one of the charges leveled against him was that he claimed to be able to tear down God's temple and build it again in three days (Matthew 26:61). This was a serious charge.

In those days blasphemy against the temple was an offence punishable by death. Moreover, this notion of destroying the temple and rebuilding it in three days was simply absurd as far as the religious leaders were concerned. "This temple has been under construction for forty-six years," they responded to Jesus, "and will you raise it up in three days?" They did not realize that the temple Jesus was talking about was his own body.

But of course, this clears up everything, does it not? Jesus was talking figuratively about the temple, not literally. Jesus was referring to himself; to his own suffering and death; to his own sacrifice for the sins of the world; to his resurrection from the dead. It is the *spiritual temple* that really matters in the question of the proper worship of God. It is just as Jesus said to the woman at the well: "The hour is coming, and is now here, when the true worshippers will worship the Father *in spirit and in truth*" (John 4:23). Neither a mountain in Samaria nor a temple in Jerusalem can define the boundaries of the true worship of God. "God is Spirit, and those who worship him must worship in spirit and truth" (John 4: 24).

What we are dealing with here is a different kind of temple, a different conception of what constitutes a 'house of God.' We are dealing with Jesus Christ himself. Jesus is the one who sets the standard for our lives and for our worship of God. It does not have to do with a place, or a building, or a tradition or a theological system or creed. It is not a matter of general consensus based on the majority of opinions of religious people. Rather, Jesus, and Jesus alone, is the one who determines the standard for our faith and for our relationship to God.

Faith in Jesus is ultimately what this story of the cleansing of the temple is about. After Jesus was raised from the dead, his disciples remembered that he had spoken this word about his body. And, as a result, "they believed the scripture and the word that Jesus had spoken" (John 2:22). This whole passage in John's gospel has to do with *believing in Jesus*. While Jesus was staying in Jerusalem for the Passover feast many people believed in his name, being amazed at the signs he was performing (John 2:23).

However, if faith in Jesus' word and trust in him personally are the main themes of this story and if holy places and holy traditions are not the most important factors for the true worship of God, then why did Jesus become so upset over the misuse of the temple building? If the true worship of God consists of worship 'in spirit and truth' and is not limited to place or ritual, then the use (or even the abuse) of these superficial institutions should really be of no consequence, should they?

As a matter of fact, the outward use or abuse of a holy institution (be it a place or a tradition) actually does matter very much. If there is something on the outside that is not quite right, then it is generally true that there is also an inward problem—a spiritual problem. Conversely, wherever there is a spiritual problem on the inside, it is bound to display itself in overt ways as well.

Some time ago, while leafing through a book containing historical photos of American architectural structures, which have fallen into ruin or been demolished over the years, I landed upon the photo of an old church building somewhere in the American south-west. The building was originally erected as a mission church in the small settlement. After the structure ceased to be used as a house of worship and up until the time when it was demolished, this church building served a variety of functions in succession. It was first used as a barn and then was converted into a hotel. Before it was finally demolished, it served for a time as a house of prostitution. Now, what does this tell us about the faith of a community, when their one-time house of worship is allowed to deteriorate into a bordello? Or (to use an example a bit closer to home), does it really matter when declining Christian groups in the post-Christian West sell their houses of worship to be used as discos, antique halls, or temples and houses of worship for people of non-Christian religions? Does this attitude to the legacy of their house of worship say anything about their own faith?

For all practical purposes the Jerusalem temple had become a market hall. We may well ask how it came to this. Why were there cattle and sheep and doves being sold in the temple courts? Why were there so many opportunists and ruthless bankers who were cashing in on the lucrative business of money changing? Actually, all these things were well meant, at least in the beginning. The people who came to the temple to worship God required sacrificial victims for their worship. Many of these worshippers lived far away from Jerusalem so that it was virtually impossible for them to bring their own animals for sacrifice. The provision for buying sacrificial animals right there in the temple courts was a type of public service. This was true also of the moneychangers. There were many worshippers who came from outside Palestine (see Acts 2:5-12) and who brought with them their foreign currencies. They had to change their money into the proper currency in order to buy their sacrificial animals and carry on business in the city of Jerusalem.

During the special religious feasts, such as the feast of the Passover, the opportunity to buy sacrificial animals in Jerusalem was particularly important. The Jewish historian Flavius Josephus, who lived and wrote during the first century AD, reports about one particular Passover feast that he had observed when over a quarter of a million lambs were slaughtered in the temple in one day. Many scholars believe that Josephus was exaggerating the total number here, but it is certain that there were a lot of animals in the temple at this time. Can we imagine the sight of so many sheep in a small, confined area? Can we imagine how it must have smelled? Can we imagine how much money was changing hands as sheep were being bought, sold, and slaughtered?

This sale of sacrificial animals was no longer simply a public service. This had grown into big business! Along with this big business there were big business people who were out to make big money at this annual festival. Any sense of public service had long since been forgotten. God's house had become a department store. The house of prayer had become a noisy, smelly stockyard.

It is not the portrayal of Jesus in this story that is inconsistent with faith. Rather, it was the outward religious practice that was inconsistent with the true worship of God. This really has very little to do with some legalistic condemnation of buying and selling in a so-called 'house of God.' This story is not about the propriety or impropriety of holding a mission bazaar in the church basement. It has nothing to do with whether or not the youth group should be allowed to sponsor a car wash in the church car park in order to raise funds for some common project. This story of the cleansing of the temple has nothing to do with such trivial questions.

Rather, it has to do with the problem of outward actions, which are inconsistent with a firm, faithful, inward relationship with God. What Jesus did that day in the temple was not in contradiction to a right relationship with God. On the contrary, Jesus' actions were in complete harmony with God's will. Later on, when the disciples reflected on this cleansing of the temple, they remembered the passage in Psalm 69:10: "Zeal for your house will consume me!"

To be sure, the prophetic word spoken by Jesus concerning his resurrection did lead the disciples to put their trust in him. But there was another word that led them to believe in Jesus. It was this word from the Psalms about Jesus' binding, burning love for the house of God that helped Jesus' followers to trust in him. This is the word of scripture to which John refers when he tells us that the disciples "believed the scripture and the word that Jesus had spoken" (John 2:22).

Jesus' cleansing of the temple has to do with faith and trust. Trust in God is never a purely private, inward phenomenon. Our inward relationship with God will display itself in our outward lives, in our actions and, above all, in our worship of God. Our love for God will consume us inwardly like a blazing fire, until it can be translated outwardly into loving, zealous action. This is the lesson we learn from the strange picture of Jesus in the cleansing of the temple; and this is an important part of what it means for us to believe in that same Jesus.

4

Human Knowledge Has Its Boundaries
John 3:1-16

WHAT DO we know about Jesus? To some people the answer to this question might seem quite obvious. We know a great deal about Jesus. One only has to read through the pages of the New Testament to see how much we know about Jesus. But precisely this question is probably one of the most debated questions among New Testament scholars today. On the one hand there are those who maintain that we can know practically nothing about the historical Jesus of Nazareth who walked upon this earth almost two thousand years ago. These scholars believe that the writings of the New Testament were so formulated by the ideas, hopes and aspirations of the early Church that the historical person of Jesus remains hopelessly hidden to us today.

On the other hand, there are many biblical scholars who firmly maintain that the New Testament writings give us an accurate picture of the historical Jesus. The early Christian authors remained true to the actual historical facts and recorded them without straying from the truth.

It is too often the case, however, that the people who maintain that they know the truth about Jesus—about who he was then and who he is today—that these people prefer to keep their knowledge hidden. They store away this precious knowledge in the shadowy recesses of the night, rather than publish openly their good news about Jesus in their own daily lives. Indeed, there is a certain risk involved in speaking too loudly, too openly or too often about Jesus. It is the risk of confrontation. It is the risk that someone else may begin to ask critical questions. The one who claims to know something about Jesus may be challenged to back up those claims. So it is that there are many Christians who prefer to keep themselves, their Christianity and their knowledge about Jesus hidden away. It is much more comfortable and it feels much more secure to keep to ourselves our opinions and our knowledge about Jesus, rather than to confess Christ openly before a watching world. This behavior is just like that of Nicodemus, who came to Jesus by night to seek an audience with him.

Nicodemus knew something about Jesus: "Rabbi," he said, "we know that you are a teacher who has come from God; for no one can do these signs that you do apart from the presence of God" (John 3:2).

Well done, Nicodemus! You deserve a high score for your theology exam! You have learned your Sunday school lessons well. You have done your homework. You are the star scholar in your local Bible study group. *You know something about Jesus!* In fact, you know something *very important* about Jesus. You know that Jesus has come from God. You know that the very hand of God is at work in the ministry of Jesus Christ. *Very good, Nicodemus! Very good!*

But this is not quite good enough, Nicodemus: "Very truly, I tell you, no one can see the kingdom of God without being born from above" (3:3). Pure human knowledge has its boundaries. Nicodemus' knowledge had its limits. There was something that Nicodemus did not know. In some ways his knowledge of Jesus was no clearer than the deep shadows of the night in which he came to speak with Jesus. Nicodemus knew something extremely significant about Jesus, but there was something even more important that he did not know. He did not know about being born from above. He did not know what it meant to participate in God's kingdom.

Come out, Nicodemus! Come out of the shadows of the night where you are hiding away with your knowledge of Jesus. *Come in* to the streaming daylight of the full knowledge of Jesus!

Come out, Nicodemus! Come out of the darkness of your silent and seemingly secure arms-length distance from Jesus. *Come in* and be confronted with the full light of the presence of Jesus Christ!

Come out, Nicodemus! Come out of the night of your uncertain, human knowledge. *Come in* to the daylight of faith in Jesus Christ!

For the light is shining in the darkness. The light has come into the world. This is the *true light*, which gives light to every man and woman. The shadowy recesses of the night of ignorance and unbelief will no longer offer any security or any comfortable distance. Now is the time to step out of the darkness and into the full light of God. Now is the time that the kingdom of God is appearing. Now is the time that important decisions must be made. *You must be born from above!*

Who? *Me? Nicodemus? I* must be born from above? There is something I do not know about? Why, that is absurd! I am a Pharisee. I live according to the strictest rules of the Holy Scriptures. I am an educated biblical scholar. I am a teacher of the Bible. I have the best theological education it is possible to get. How is it that there is something important that I am unaware of?

I am one of the rulers of the Jews and I hold a position of great responsibility among God's people. I am a faithful member of the church; I was brought into the church when I was just a baby; my parents and grandparents and great-grandparents were all faithful members; I was brought up in the church and taught in the church and confirmed in the church. Now someone is telling me that *I* am lacking in knowledge in some way—that *I* must be born from above? This is simply absurd—just as absurd as the notion that an old man could enter into his mother's womb and be born a second time!

"How can this be?" asked Nicodemus.

Ah, wait a minute, Nicodemus. What was that you said just now?

"How can this be?"

One more time, Nicodemus, what was your question?

"How can this be?"

Oh, Nicodemus, you mean to say that there *is* something that you do not know—something you do not understand? "Very truly, I tell you," explained Jesus, "no one can enter the kingdom of God without being born of water and Spirit. What is born of the flesh is flesh, and what is born of the Spirit is spirit. Do not be astonished that I said to you, 'You must be born from above'" (3:5-7).

Simply to know something about Jesus is not sufficient for people who want to enter God's kingdom—not even if it is something *important* that they know about Jesus. *Knowledge* of Jesus must be tied together with *acknowledgement* of Jesus. People can never truly, fully *know* Jesus until they *acknowledge* Jesus as Lord and Christ and until they commit themselves to him.

This personal commitment to Jesus is precisely what was lacking for Nicodemus. Of course, Nicodemus could have gained much from further theological reflection; he could have learned more about Jesus and gained more knowledge and experience. But without personal commitment to Jesus, even this further exercise would have been of little benefit to him. Simply the fact that he came to Jesus by night was an indication of the cautious distance he wished to maintain between himself and Jesus.

To be born from above is not simply a matter of learning something about Jesus and agreeing with historical statements of fact. Being born from above is a matter of acknowledging Jesus and making a personal commitment to him through faith and faithful living. It means to step out of the shadows and into the light, leaving behind the cautious 'arms-length distance' position. It means to put into practice what is known about Jesus by making a life-encompassing commitment to him; by being baptized in his name; by receiving the gift of his Holy Spirit; by taking hold of the new life, the eternal life, which Jesus alone can offer.

Pure human knowledge has its boundaries. "The wind blows where it chooses, and you hear the sound of it, but *you do not know,* Nicodemus, where it comes from or where it goes. So it is with everyone who is born of the Spirit" (3:8).

While living in Germany I coined the expression *Sonntagseinkäufer*—'Sunday Shoppers'—to refer to a national pastime for Sunday afternoons. Sunday trading was, and still is, virtually non-existent in Germany and rigidly controlled by law. But a favorite Sunday afternoon activity for many was to take a stroll through the pedestrian zones of shopping streets and simply to window-shop. The businesses in these districts would cater to the Sunday afternoon guests by arranging interesting displays in their entryways, as well as in their storefront windows. Indeed, window-shopping is a very comfortable and non-committal way to go shopping, particularly if you are a student and have no money! Moreover, a 'Sunday shopper' can really know a lot of consumer information—the latest fashions, prices, sales and special offers, etc. But unless the 'Sunday shopper' goes back into the city on Monday morning and hands over the cash at the till, he or she will always be missing out on the most important knowledge of all. The person who is only a window-shopper is always an outsider with a mass of information, which is of no tangible, personal benefit.

This was Nicodemus' problem. He knew that there was something special about Jesus. He could feel the wind blowing; he could sense the movement of God's Spirit. But where was it coming from? Where was it going? This, he did not know, because in spite of all that he did know about Jesus, he was still an outsider. He had not yet made a personal life-commitment to Jesus.

At the end, Nicodemus admitted his ignorance. "How can these things be?" he asked Jesus (3:9).

"What?" Jesus replied (perhaps with a bit of sarcasm!). "Are you a teacher of Israel, and yet you do not understand these things? We speak of what we know and testify to what we have seen" (3:10-11). What is your problem, Nicodemus, that you do not know?

Your problem, Nicodemus, is that you do not receive our testimony. You do not take Jesus seriously. You refuse to commit yourself to him. Your problem is that you refuse to change your life around and acknowledge Jesus as

Lord. Your problem, Nicodemus, is that you prefer to stay hidden in the shadows, at a cautious distance from Jesus. Your problem, Nicodemus, is that you have not put your faith, your trust in Jesus Christ!

"I have told you about earthly things and you do not believe, how can you believe if I tell you about heavenly things?" asked Jesus (3:12).

Believing in Jesus Christ is what transforms *knowledge* about Jesus into *acknowledgement* of Jesus. Faith is the life-encompassing commitment to Jesus as Lord and Savior. It is through faith that new birth takes place, the birth which is from above, effected by water and Spirit, the birth which issues forth into new life, into *eternal life*.

For Nicodemus and for people today, the difference between knowledge without faith and knowledge bound together with faith is like the difference between night and day, between dark shadows and broad daylight. Believing in Jesus is the key to true knowledge about Jesus.

What then do we know about Jesus today? We truly do know a great deal. We know that Jesus is a teacher who has come from God, for no one could do the miraculous signs that he does unless God is at work in him. We know that Jesus is the Son of Man who came down from heaven and who has ascended again to the right hand of the Father. We know that Jesus is the one who has conquered death. We know that Jesus is the only begotten Son of God and that everyone who believes in him will inherit eternal life. There are many more very important things that we know about Jesus.

But there is more to being a Christian than obtaining knowledge. There is also commitment. Knowledge alone will not allow us to participate in God's kingdom. Faith in Jesus Christ belongs inseparably to knowledge about him.

Now is the moment that the Kingdom of God has come near. Now is the time when important decisions must be made. You must be born from above; you must be born of water and Spirit. Our knowledge about Christ must not be isolated from a faithful commitment to Christ. "For God so loved the world that he gave his only Son, so that everyone who *believes in him* may not perish but may have eternal life" (3:16).

5

Snakes in the Desert
John 3:14-21

I AM NOT generally attracted to stories about snakes. Actually, from my early childhood I have had a very strong aversion to snakes or anything having to do with them—an aversion undoubtedly inherited from my mother! Whenever I see a snake, I immediately get cold chills up and down my back; and I saw a lot of snakes when I was a child, growing up on a farm in central Illinois.

I try to avoid any and all contact with snakes, even when there is no danger of direct contact. It takes a great deal of will power for me to visit the reptile house at the zoo or to watch a wildlife documentary on television. The main problem I have with snakes is that they never really go away; they simply hide. They slink and slither around in our subconscious until that moment when our defences are low. Then, suddenly, in the middle of the night, when we are sleeping soundly and quietly, they pop up in a nightmare and scare us half to death! Cutting through all the complexities of Freudian analysis, my point is simply this: I don't like snakes!

I imagine that it must have been pretty horrible to wander through a desert and be attacked by a brood of poisonous snakes. This is what the people of Israel experienced during their wilderness wanderings. This is the background event in John's gospel (3:14-21) when Jesus talks about Moses lifting up the snake in the wilderness. Numbers 21:4-9 provides the account about the Israelites and their passage through the wilderness after the exodus from Egypt. On this particular occasion the people became impatient and dissatisfied. They complained to God and to Moses, "Why have you brought us up out of Egypt to die in the wilderness? For there is no food and no water, and we detest this miserable [manna]!" (Numbers 21:5).

Because of the ingratitude and dissension among the people, the Lord sent poisonous snakes among them. Many Israelites were bitten by the snakes and died as a result. When this began to happen, the people very quickly changed their tone. They came to Moses and cried out: "We have sinned by speaking against the Lord and against you" (Numbers 21:7). They pleaded with Moses to intercede on their behalf so that they would be spared.

The Lord answered Moses' prayer of intercession by instructing him to fashion a snake and to raise it up on a pole so that the Israelites could see it. Anyone who had been bitten could look toward this snake on the pole and be saved from the poisonous bite. Moses followed these instructions. He molded a snake out of bronze and fastened it on a pole. Everyone who looked up at the bronze snake was saved.

Although I normally shy away from snake stories, I find this incident in the book of Numbers most interesting. This story relates how God was saving men and women from what would have been certain death. Moreover, God was saving the people of Israel from the inevitable consequences of their own sin against him. Let us review the main story line. The Israelites had rebelled against God and against Moses. The punishment for this rebellion was the bite of death from a venomous serpent. As the people were in the throes of death, they cried out to God for salvation and deliverance. At the first sign of this repentance God responded to their cries by setting up a provision for salvation. The ones who trusted God by lifting up their eyes to God's provision of salvation were spared, in spite of the deadly snakebite.

This story about Moses and the bronze snake is a story about salvation. It is a part of the bigger story of how God, in his infinite love and compassion, delivers men and women from their sins and saves them from death. This deliverance does not occur as a result of magic or of some sort of 'hocus-pocus.' Rather, this salvation is a direct result of the love of God. Later on in Israel's history there developed a tendency amongst the people to put their trust in magic charms. Eventually even this bronze snake that Moses fashioned became the object of superstitious worship among the Israelites. 2 Kings 18 reports that Hezekiah, a God-fearing king who cleansed the land of Judah from idol worship, had to destroy this bronze snake because the Israelites had set it up as an idol. They were worshipping it and burning incense before it. They named it: "The Bronze God."

This was obviously not what God intended when he provided salvation for the Israelites at the time of Moses. Their deliverance from the poisonous snakes did not occur through the magic powers of a good-luck charm, but through the grace and power of God alone. The author of the Old Testament apocryphal book of Wisdom of Solomon understood this very clearly to be the case. In the form of a prayer to God, this devout believer wrote about this salvation story in the book of Numbers in the following words:

> For when the terrible rage of wild animals came
> upon your people and they were being destroyed
> by the bites of writhing serpents, your wrath did
> not continue to the end; they were troubled for
> a little while as a warning, and received a symbol
> of deliverance to remind them of your law's com-
> mand. For the one who turned towards it was
> saved, not by the thing that was beheld, but by
> you, the Savior of all. . . . But your children were
> not conquered even by the fangs of venomous
> serpents, for your mercy came to their help and
> healed them. . . . For neither herb nor poultice
> cured them, but it was your word, O Lord, that
> heals all people. (Wisdom of Solomon 16:5-12)

The story about Moses and the snake in the wilderness is a salvation story. As such, it is a small fragment of
the *complete* salvation story of God, which takes place in
the person and work of Jesus Christ. "Just as Moses lifted
up the serpent in the wilderness, so must the Son of Man
be lifted up, *that whoever believes in him may have eternal
life*" (John 3:14-15). God's complete and perfect plan of
salvation is present in Jesus Christ. Jesus was not 'lifted up'
on the cross so that a few, select men and women might
be saved, but so that all people might find their way to
God. Jesus did not die on the cross to save people from
poisonous snakebites, but to rescue them from a worse
form of death.

All the people of the world stand guilty before God.
All people have rebelled against the Lord, as the Israelites
did in the desert. All people have sinned, and the punishment for this sin is the same as for the Israelites when they
rebelled. That punishment is certain death! Apart from
intimate fellowship with God, there is no possibility of
life, for God is the source of life. Anyone who, through
the rebellion of sin, rejects that fellowship with God is

effectively rejecting the only possibility for life. These are people who are without God; and people who are without God are without the hope of life. The only thing certain for them is death.

But the situation need not be hopeless. There is good news in this story. God so loved the world, that he gave his only Son, so that everyone who looks to him and believes in him will not perish through death, but will have eternal life (see John 3:16)! This is good news in an otherwise bleak situation. The situation of men and women who have sinned is not a hopeless situation! God, in his eternal love, has provided an escape, a new *exodus*, from sin and certain death. Jesus Christ came into this world of sin and death; he was lifted up on the cross to die for the sins of the world; he was raised victorious from the dead and offers eternal life to all the people in the world!

The story of Jesus Christ is the genuine, complete and perfect story of the salvation and deliverance that God offers to the world. People who entrust their lives to this same Jesus enter into the scene and become another part of the story of salvation. Whoever believes in Jesus has eternal life. Whoever believes in Jesus does not perish through death. Whoever believes in Jesus will not even be judged or condemned on account of his or her own sin. "Indeed, God did not send the son into the world to condemn the world, but in order that the world might be saved through him" (3:17).

Jesus did not come to judge the world; but that does not mean that there is no judgment. Apart from Jesus, apart from faith and trust in him, there is no alternative but judgment. "Those who do not believe are condemned already, because they have not believed in the name of the only Son of God" (3:18).

This is perhaps a bit hard to believe, is it not? God breaks into the history of the world and tells a new story. It is a story whereby lost, hopeless, dying men and women are offered a way out of their certain death situation and a way into eternal life. The only thing that these people have to do is to accept this provision of God. All they have to do is to cast their eyes upward—upward to the Son of God who was lifted up on a cross for their sins and then raised up from the dead for their deliverance. So simple is the salvation that God offers to men and women today; it is as simple as for the Israelites who only needed to cast their glance up to the bronze snake and live.

But in spite of God's provision of salvation, there is still judgment and condemnation. "The light has come into the world, and people loved darkness rather than the light because their deeds were evil" (3:19). As inconceivable as it seems, there is still judgment, and there is still condemnation, because there are still people who reject Jesus. As inconceivable as it seems, there were Israelites who died of snakebites in the desert. How unnecessary was their death! All they had to do was to look to God for his provision of life. It was so terribly *simple!*

Still there were men and women who died. Was it because they were stubborn? Was it because of their hardheartedness or their vain human pride? Yes, it was surely because of all these things. But also, as inconceivable as it seems to me and to people who share my aversion to snakes, there are simply people who like snakes; there are people who like to play around with poisonous serpents. There are people who like to toy with death. There are people who like to play around with sin. There are people who despise the mercy of God, instead of trusting in him and accepting his provision of salvation. This is a dangerous and foolish game, for it involves a rejection of the glorious and free offer of salvation from the living and loving God.

Such foolishness can only result in judgment and condemnation. But everyone who believes in Jesus is spared the judgment and the condemnation. People who believe in Jesus will not perish through death, but will have eternal life!

6

A Thirsty Woman
Finds Living Water
John 4:1-30

THE DAY began just like every other day in the village of Sychar in Samaria. A nameless woman—a woman about whom we know nothing, except for what we read in John, chapter 4—went to Jacob's well outside of town to fetch water. The day was just like hundreds and thousands of other normal, predictable, uneventful, drudgery days that this woman had experienced: Get up in the morning; make the bed; brush your teeth; prepare breakfast; send the husband off to work and the kids off to school; clean the house; pick up something at the market for lunch; *and don't forget to fetch the water!*

Fetching the water was not a nice chore for a woman to have to do. It was not a nice chore for *anyone* to have to do! Fetching water was a laborious task. There was no modern convenience of running water in the house. There was not even an aqueduct running through the village to provide fresh water at the street corner. All of the water for all of the daily needs—for washing, cooking and drinking—had to be drawn daily from the well outside of town and transported in large, heavy clay pots.

This was an inconvenient chore, a tedious chore, a physically exhausting chore, and above all, *a woman's chore!* So it was that this nameless woman on this nameless day went out to Jacob's well to bring in the water, just as she had done perhaps 10,000 times before. Little did she know that on this particular day she would bring home a different kind of water!

Just thinking about the situation in modern terms we might ask ourselves the question why this woman even bothered. Why did she go thousands and thousands of times in the course of her lifetime to perform this tiring, thankless chore? Why did she go out on this particular day? Why could she not simply skip a day, take the day off and have a little holiday from the work? Why not?

The answer, quite simply, is that she was thirsty! Water is necessary for life. In a land where it is hot and dry, people always have to take care that there is enough water to drink. I remember clearly those hot days of late July and early August in central Illinois when, as a child on the farm, I would have to join my Dad and my brothers, walking the rows of soybeans and cutting out the weeds. I remember the burning sun and the feeling of thirst. I remember the eager anticipation, after turning back at the end of a long row of soybeans, of reaching the jug of ice-cold water waiting for us back at the opposite end of the field.

I remember hot summer Sunday evenings at church, in the days before air-conditioning, when the preacher would be going on and on with a sermon. All the ladies and children in the church were using whatever they could find in the pews to fan themselves: old printed programs or church newsletters. The really fortunate ones might have had one of those purpose-made pew fans—a piece of cardboard on a wooden stick, printed with a religious scene on the front and an advertisement for the local funeral home on the back! Often the preacher would stop in the middle of the sermon, reach down into the pulpit and produce a glass of water. He would then mercilessly proceed to guzzle the water in the full view of this congregation of men and women and children who were also dying of thirst! Everybody gets thirsty, every day of their lives!

The Samaritan woman was thirsty. That is why she went with her clay water jug to Jacob's well outside the town to draw water. She was thirsty. Every day she got thirsty. Time and time again throughout the day she got thirsty. On this particular day it was around noon when she went to the well and up to this point it had likely been a perfectly normal day. It is possible that she met a group of Jewish men on her way to the well, about twelve in all. This was a bit out of the ordinary since Jews tended to go out of their way in order to avoid traveling through the country of Samaria. But these men would have kept their distance from her, not wanting to have anything to do with her. This too would have been normal, for the Jews and the Samaritans shared a mutual hatred of each other. Moreover, she was a *woman*, and it was not customary for men to address or to have contact with women in public.

However, when she arrived at the well she found another Jewish man. He too was thirsty after his morning travels. But the well was deep and he did not have a bucket or jar or anything else that he could use to draw water. As the woman came near, the Jewish man spoke to her, asking for a drink of water.

This was no longer a normal, routine day! What did this Jewish man want from this Samaritan woman? Was he trying to frighten her in some way? Was he trying to harass her or to have some fun at her expense? At any rate (so the woman must have thought), he did not simply want a drink of water. An upright, religious Jew would rather die of thirst before he would ask a Samaritan woman for a drink of water!

This was now an abnormal situation. What should the woman do? How should she react? The best thing to do, she thought, is to try to get the water as quickly as possible, deal with this Jewish man in short shrift and get on her way back home. "You are a Jewish man," she replied curtly, "and I am a Samaritan woman. We have nothing to do with each other."

But that was not the end of the story. The man spoke to her again: "If you knew the gift of God, and who it is that is saying to you, 'Give me a drink', then you would have asked him, and he would have given you *living water*" (John 4:10).

"Oh, so now he wants to give *me* something", thought the woman—"*living water*." The woman knew, of course, what living water is. Living water is the opposite of still water that one would expect to find in a pond or in a lake or at the surface of a well, such as Jacob's well. Living water is water that is flowing and rushing, water falling from a high cliff, water flowing rapidly in a brook or stream, water gushing forth from an underground spring. Still water becomes easily foul, full of algae, bacteria and covered with scum. Living water, on the other hand, is fresh, clean, clear, sparkling and healthy. When presented with the choice, anyone would naturally prefer to drink living water.

But there was really no choice in this situation. Jacob's well was deep and this Jewish man did not even have a bucket to draw the still water from the surface of the well. Who did this man think he was? Did he think that he was greater than the patriarch Jacob, the grandson of Abraham, who dug this well in the first place? Where did he think he was going to get living water? So the woman decided to call his bluff on this issue.

But the Jewish man was not put off. "Everyone who drinks of this water will be thirsty again," he continued, "but those who drink of the water that I will give will never be thirsty. The water I will give will become in them a spring of water gushing up to eternal life" (4:13-14).

What a fine idea, the woman must have thought—water that she could drink and never get thirsty again! "Sir," she said (perhaps with a strong note of sarcasm in her voice), "give me this water, and then I will never have to come back to this well and perform this tiring chore again!" But then came the decisive moment of the story.

"Go, call your husband, and come back," said the man.

"I have no husband," replied the woman.

"You are right in saying 'I have no husband,'" the Jewish man continued, "for you have had five husbands and the one you have now is not your husband." Yes, the woman was telling the truth!

With this word from Jesus the whole matter became deadly serious for the woman. The mask she was wearing and the facade she was trying to project were now suddenly removed. A Samaritan woman who was thirsty for life stood before Jesus, stripped of all her excuses and pretences, with all of her faults and failures and sins exposed.

This Samaritan woman had a thirst, which the water from Jacob's well could not quench. Her life itself was proof that she was thirsty for something that she had not yet been able to find. Just the fact that she had come to the well alone and at this hour of the day was proof that there was something wrong, something missing in her life. (The women of a village normally went to fetch water in groups and in the cooler hours of the morning or evening.) As a matter of fact, there was something vital missing in this woman's life. She was missing out on a firm relationship with God.

But this is precisely the point that she did not wish to concede. She did not want to admit to herself or to anyone else that she needed God. She wanted to quench her thirst for life all on her own and with her own reserves. So she tried to quench her thirst for life through a marital relationship. "If only I can make this marriage work," she thought to herself, "then I will have everything I want." But she failed; it did not work out. Well, perhaps she had married the wrong man. So she tried marriage with another man; and then another man; and then another man; and with another man. Five times she was married, and five times she was still coming up short, thirsting for life. She even tried to quench her thirst for life through an extra-marital relationship. But that was no better. She tried further, as many people do, to quench her thirst for life by getting a little religion. She had worshipped God with the other Samaritan people on Mt. Gerazim in Samaria. But that was a misguided attempt at being religious, and she always came away from this experience still thirsty for life.

The Samaritan woman still had one more hope, however. There was one more possibility for quenching her thirst for life. "I know that Messiah is coming," she said. This was the great, last hope. When Messiah comes, he will tell us all things. He will quench our thirst for life. We will never be thirsty again.

"I am he, the one who is speaking to you," Jesus answered (4:26).

To this very day there are women and men who are thirsty for life—people who are searching on their own for joy and happiness and fulfillment in life, but without a firm and consequent relationship with God. If only I had a different wife. . . . If only I had married a different man. . . . If only I had a different job. . . . If only I had a different boss. . . . If only I could move and live in a different place. . . . If only I could get a better education. . . . If only I were in a different church. . . . If only I had better health. . . . If only I had more money, or more of *this* or more of *that*. . . . *If only I.* . . .

But people will never be rid of their thirst for life until they give up playing this game of "if only I." They will never find satisfaction until they lay aside all their masks and pretences, until they stand before Jesus Christ, with all their excuses, their faults, their failures and their sins laid bare before him, and they ask *Jesus* for a drink of living water.

The Samaritan woman received a drink of living water from Jesus that very day. Suddenly the water of Jacob's well was no longer so important to her. She left her water jar there at the well. She did not even bother to draw any water from the well. She ran back into town and proclaimed to the people there: "Come and see a man who told me everything I have ever done! He cannot be the Messiah, can he?"

Yes, as a matter of fact, Jesus *is* Messiah, the Christ, and the promised Savior of the world. Anyone who comes to Jesus today, believing in him and simply asking from him—that person will also receive from Jesus a drink of living water. Just as for the Samaritan woman, so for people today, the living water that Jesus gives will be like a mighty spring gushing forth in their soul, quenching their thirst for life and granting eternal life.

7

People Need a Holiday
John 6:1-15

FESTIVALS AND holidays are truly important for all people everywhere. Without the holidays that pop up at regular and predictable intervals in our year-to-year routines, the pressures of the daily grind would be almost unbearable. Everyone needs a time off from work in order to rest and to pursue refreshing forms of recreation. We all need the change of pace from normal routine, which our most special holidays allow us. We need the opportunity to celebrate, because life is more than work and human beings are not machines.

Our religious, Christian holidays are particularly important. These special days in the church calendar point out very clearly to us, and in a way that other secular celebrations are unable to point out, that there is another, more important dimension to human life than the day-to-day rat race. There is a divine dimension, a spiritual dimension to our lives here on earth. Especially because of this dimension we have reason to celebrate.

When my wife and I first moved to Germany at the beginning of my doctoral studies, we were deeply impressed by the fact that almost all of the public holidays were Christian holidays that were taken directly from the church calendar. Not only were the regular holidays of Christmas and Easter included, but also Epiphany, Good Friday, Easter Monday, Pentecost Sunday and Monday, Ascension Day, Corpus Christi, etc. As Christians, it meant a great deal to us to be able to celebrate these Christian festivals with the peace and quiet of time off from the normal routine of life and work.

It is, however, unfortunate that regular holidays and even Christian holidays can simply become a part of the normal routine. Instead of directing our thoughts and activities to something different, to something more, our holidays often become just another part of our daily grind that we simply take for granted. I quickly observed in Germany that there was only a small percentage of the population that actually reflected on the deeper, religious meaning of the holidays they celebrated. In spite of the efforts of the Church, most people on the streets had absolutely no clue as to the original meaning of the religious holidays or what they commemorated.

When this is the case, it is very easy then for the worries, stresses and problems of everyday life to invade the sacred realm of holiday time and rob the holiday of its own special meaning and cause for celebration. A good example of this is what we see happening on an ever-increasing scale to the holiday season of Advent and Christmas. Advent is a time for celebration, joy, and glad anticipation because of the expected coming of the Lord. People should be caught up with celebration because they are reminded about how God sent his Son into the world.

But what is it that so many people experience during this time, in increasing measure? *Stress!* There is so much human 'busyness' in this season that many people never get around to thinking about the divine business, which provided the holiday in the first place. People are filled with concerns and worries. Will the whole family be able to gather together, all at the same place and at the same time? Will our bank accounts be able to provide for all the necessary gifts for all the family members and friends on our shopping list? Will this season be as good for the wholesalers and retailers as it was last year, or should they begin the big push for the Christmas shopping season a few days earlier than last year?

This is not to say that it is a sin when people do not celebrate a religious holiday as a religious holiday. That would be far too trite. After all, my own national heritage, which calls for separation of church and state, actually dictates that most of the special holidays of the church calendar have no legal holiday status. Even those holidays, which are allowed legal status (such as Christmas and Easter), must find their rationale as holidays in purely non-religious terms. At the end of the day, there really is nothing particularly 'holy' in any one day over against another day. (This is a view which has some merit, but which has been taken to extremes in certain non-conformist movements!)

Yet, people really do need holidays. People need festivals and celebrations and commemorations that free them from the routine of day-to-day life and point them to something more important.

"Now the Passover, the festival of the Jews, was near" (John 6:4). There was a crowd of people who had followed after Jesus because they had seen how he healed the sick. These very people should have been making preparations for their annual religious festival which was now just around the corner. They should have been preparing their hearts and minds for this commemoration and celebration. It was a festival of deliverance, a feast of liberation, a celebration of the faithfulness and trustworthiness of the grace and love of their God. They should have been remembering how, long ago, the blood of the Passover lamb had been smeared on the doorposts of the Israelite homes in Egypt to protect the people inside from death. They should have been thinking about how difficult and bitter it was for their ancestors to be slaves in Egypt. They should have been rejoicing and celebrating as they remembered how God freed their nation from slavery and led them with a mighty hand out of Egypt. That was the meaning of this imminent Passover feast. Such a commemoration, such a holiday, such a celebration of liberation was precisely what these people needed so badly at this time in their history.

But there were so many external stresses they had to deal with. There were traffic jams and long delays on the major highways because of the holiday traffic with people heading south to relax in the sun. There were political crises at home and abroad, with corruption in high public offices. There were economic troubles, and no one was sure that they would have enough money to take a holiday from work. There was unrest within the family, and they were not sure that they would be able to have a big, happy get-together, the way 'mama and papa always wanted it to be.' There was poverty in the land. There were epidemics of illness and disease. There was hunger and thirst, at home and in various parts of the world. The everyday routine, with all its problems, concerns and stresses, had become a prison cell for these people. Even a holiday of deliverance was not enough to free them from this prison.

As a matter of fact, they were unable to envision any kind of liberation from the issues weighing on their minds. They were not interested in a Passover lamb to take away the sins of the world and to bring freedom from their bondage to sin. They were more interested in a king, who would break the yoke of a foreign government and establish a new, earthly kingdom of Israel. These people did not care about a Passover lamb whose vicarious death would mean life for them. They wanted instead a miracle worker who would multiply bread to fill their empty stomachs. They wanted a prophet like Elisha, who on one occasion fed a hundred hungry men with only twenty small loaves of bread, with the result that everyone had more than enough to eat. These people in the story of John chapter six wanted the kind of prophet who would direct his attention to satisfying the everyday hunger in the lives of everyday people—and who would do this every day! Of course, it would be wonderful if all of this could take place within the framework of the great national festival of Passover, right in the midst of their everyday experience!

But the people's everyday lives had become a prison cell. In their yearning for liberation from the foreign rule of the Romans, they had ceased to grasp the fact that there was a more oppressive foreign dictator ruling in their lives—the cruel slavemaster of sin. In their striving for bread to satisfy their empty stomachs, they had grown insensitive to the fact that there is a deeper kind of hunger, a worse danger of starvation, which can only be remedied by 'bread from heaven.'

The Passover festival season that was now upon them should have been a celebration of freedom and deliverance. But they remained shackled in the chains of their everyday existence. The day was drawing near when they would slaughter lambs in the temple, but no one was mindful of the lives that would be saved through the shedding of the blood of the Lamb of God. They ate bread in the desert, a place where bread is normally not plentiful. But they did eat; they were satisfied, and they even had leftovers. They realized immediately that a miracle had taken place. But no one gave pause to think about the deeper hunger, which even this miraculous bread could not satisfy.

And so Jesus withdrew by himself into the mountains.

The Passover Feast of the Jews was drawing near, and Jesus knew what lay before him at this national feast. Jesus had not come to be the miracle-working prophet that the people wanted him to be. He had not come to be the kind of king that they were expecting. Rather, Jesus approached this Passover feast as the Lamb of God who takes away the sins of the world. Jesus presented himself as the sacrificial Passover Lamb of God whose blood would save and preserve the lives of men and women who believed in him.

Also in the context of this miracle of the feeding of the five thousand, just prior to the Passover feast, Jesus was revealing himself to these people in the desert as God's pure and spotless Passover lamb. These people, whose hunger Jesus satisfied with five loaves of bread and two fish, were all in dire need of a holiday. They needed a real celebration. They needed a festival, a feast of freedom and liberation. They needed a festival of liberation from the foreign reign of sin in their lives. They needed a festival of liberation from the bondage of this cruel dictator. They needed a festival of liberation from the prison of their everyday life, with all its expectations, frustrations, fears and disappointments. They needed a festival of new life in the freedom that only God could provide. Because of this, whether they recognized it or not, what they really needed at this Passover feast was Jesus Christ, the Lamb of God who takes away the sins of the world.

People today have the very same need of this kind of holiday. People today need a holiday celebration that frees them from their everyday existence and points them to something more significant than the cares and crises and problems and stresses of their day-to-day lives. Men and women today need the very same liberation from the foreign dictator of sin, just as much those five thousand men and women did, who ate from the five loaves and two small fishes in the desert. Men and women today, whether they realize it or not, are just as much in need of the new life which comes only through the sacrifice of God's pure and perfect Passover Lamb. People today need a holiday. Even Christians need a holiday to celebrate the liberation they have experienced through Jesus Christ.

This is the reason why people all over the world who believe in Jesus gather together every week. They come together to celebrate with joy and thanksgiving their feast of freedom in the presence of God and his Lamb who takes away the sins of the world. In John's account of the miraculous feeding of the five thousand we read: "Then Jesus took the loaves, and when he had given thanks, he distributed them to those who were seated" (6:11). Does this not sound very similar to the words that believers call to mind in their celebrations of deliverance, which they call 'the Lord's Supper'? Indeed, in John's gospel the institution of the Lord's Supper is connected with the feeding of the five thousand and Jesus' discourse about the bread of life, rather than with the last supper in Jerusalem, as in the other gospel accounts.

Whenever Christians assemble to celebrate this feast they are participating in a holiday celebration. It is a feast of liberation from the cares and stresses of day-to-day existence. It is a feast of freedom from sin and from death. It is a celebration of new life for those who believe in Jesus. It is a celebration of thanksgiving for Jesus Christ, the Lamb of God whose blood was shed to bring life to the world. It is a celebration of remembrance that the greater, deeper hunger that all people experience can only be satisfied by God's bread, Jesus Christ.

8

Bread and Life
John 6:47-51

From the earliest beginnings of human history bread and life have belonged inseparably together. Bread, the most basic staple, serves to continue life; and life itself serves to produce and re-produce bread. "Only by toil will you eat the plants of the field all the days of your life," God said to Adam after his disobedience. "By the sweat of your face you shall eat bread until you return to the ground, for out of it you were taken" (Genesis 3:18). Down to the present day we are still living in the midst of this story of bread and life. Bread is the minister of life; life is the minister of bread. It is a natural world order, which we simply learn to take for granted.

But bread and life are anything but absolute 'givens' in our world and in our own personal experience. We want to take bread and life for granted. We want simply to count on the natural, ongoing flow of existence. We want to take for granted that we will wake up in the morning from our sleep, that we will have a couple slices of bread to pop into the toaster for our breakfast and that life simply keeps going on and on.

Personally, I have never experienced a time when I have wanted for either plenty of bread or plenty of life. This is the experience of most Christians living in the affluent West. Certainly there are plenty of differences between the kinds of bread and the standards of life, which one may experience from place to place in the lands where capitalism has become entrenched as a way of life. I recall when I first moved to Germany and was totally fascinated by the all the breads on offer in the local bakeries. In America, one has to be pretty well satisfied with either white bread or brown bread—cut into slices, wrapped in plastic bags, mushy, tasteless and with about as much nutritional value as a necktie! But in Germany there were all sorts of bread: soy bread, whole grain bread, rye bread, peasant bread, sunflower seed bread, mountain climber bread—even jogging bread! There was bread for every taste and for every occasion; and there was a bakery on every street corner (so it seemed to an extremely impressionable student fresh from the Midwestern United States!). The first day after my wife and I moved into our apartment in Tübingen, our landlords brought us the traditional gift of bread and salt—everything necessary for life—and there was plenty more where that came from!

For those of us who have learned to take for granted the everyday 'given' of bread on our tables, there is often the further tendency that we simply take for granted the daily 'given' of life itself. As long as there is plenty of bread around, we naturally assume that life will go on, and we often refuse to acknowledge that death has any power. We do not want to hear about death or dying; we do not want to talk about it; we do not even want to think about it. Just as we take for granted the sheer abundance of our daily bread, so we expect that day-to-day life is a right to be claimed.

If we are not careful, however, we are in danger of falling prey to a grave deception. Bread is indeed the minister of life and life the minister of bread. Bread is an important facilitator and pre-requisite for the continuance of human life and existence. But bread alone is not life; it is merely "pro-life." In order to serve the continuance of life and living, bread must be appropriated. That is, bread must be given and taken; it must be eaten and digested. As much as we may like to, we cannot take for granted that every man, woman and child in the world will have access today to the bread they need for the continuation of life. Neither can we take for granted that every person in the world who has access to the necessary bread is able to receive and appropriate this basic staple for physical nourishment and continued life. Some bodies are simply too unhealthy, plagued by disease which prevents life-giving bread from accomplishing its pro-life service. In the world, children and women and men die daily. The poor and hungry of the world lose their battle for life because there is no bread on their table. The sick and aged of the world lose their battle for life, often in spite of the abundance of bread. At the end of the day, people do not live by bread alone.

In John 6:47-51 Jesus speaks of bread and life both as precious gifts of God. These words of Jesus find their immediate significance in the context of the feeding of the five thousand, a story that is very familiar to Christians. Jesus crossed over the Sea of Galilee in a boat with his disciples and landed in a place that was uninhabited. It was an attempt on their part to get away for a little rest and relaxation. But a crowd of people, intent on seeing Jesus and hearing his teaching, followed them on land, walking around the coastline to the place where Jesus landed with the disciples. Jesus was moved by the crowd's hunger for his words. He was also moved by their physical hunger and the lack of resources there in the wilderness. He wanted to give the people something to eat, but all that the disciples had with them was five loaves of bread and two fish. The disciples were perplexed by the whole situation. Jesus, however, took what they had—the bread and the fish; he gave thanks to God for those good gifts of food and distributed them amongst the great crowd of people until all five thousand had eaten and were completely satisfied. On the next day, after Jesus had secretly returned to Capernaum in the night, the crowd of people sought him out once more. When they finally caught up with him, Jesus addressed them in this way: "Very truly, I tell you, you are looking for me, not because you saw signs, but because you ate your fill of the loaves."

For these people, bread was in no way a 'given' in life. Bread was not something they took for granted. Life was a constant struggle for them. They were poor people; they were racked by illness; they knew what it meant to be hungry, afraid, and anxious. They followed Jesus back and forth around the Sea of Galilee, walking on foot and searching diligently, simply for the sake of a morsel of bread—for the sake of another day of life! Jesus gave them bread. He provided enough bread for every man, woman, and child to eat their fill. There was more bread than they themselves could consume. In this giving of bread, Jesus was giving them another day of life. It was a day of salvation! Bread and life were precious gifts for the poor people of the land.

What is more, these people understood clearly from their own scriptures that bread and life are precious gifts from the hand of God. The classic instance from their history, of course, was the miraculous feeding of the Israelites in the desert with manna from heaven. Following Israel's exodus from slavery in Egypt, and all throughout the forty years of wandering in the wilderness, God provided continuous saving acts for them. God provided streams of fresh water in a dry, barren desert; God gave them meat to eat in the form of quail; and God sent them bread from heaven. In these daily acts of salvation God gave his people everything they needed for life.

"Do not fool yourselves," Jesus said to the crowds. "It was not Moses who gave you the bread from heaven, but it is my Father who gives you the true bread from heaven. For the bread of God is that which comes down from heaven and gives life to the world" (6:32-33).

"Give us this bread always," they exclaimed!

"I am the bread of life," Jesus replied. "Whoever comes to me will never be hungry and whoever believes in me will never be thirsty" (6:35).

"I am the bread of life. Whoever believes has eternal life" (6:47).

"I am the bread of life. Your ancestors ate the manna in the wilderness, and they died. This is the bread that comes down from heaven, so that one may eat of it and not die" (6:49-50).

"I am the living bread that came down from heaven. Whoever eats of this bread will live forever; and the bread that I will give for the life of the world is my flesh" (6:51).

Jesus Christ is the Bread of Life! Of course, this is something that all Christians know and affirm. True life is found only in Jesus Christ and in his word. This is something that Christians in the West have simply learned to take for granted. If it is true that Jesus is the bread of life, then one might say that the West—with its rich Christian heritage—has a 'bakery on every corner'! How else are we to understand all the beautiful church buildings and cathedrals throughout Europe? How else are we to interpret the multiplication of denominations and their presence in every town, village and city in America? Are these not the 'bakeries' that produce the bread of life for the world today—bread of life in all the different forms and shapes and combinations for every individual taste? People are baptized; they are confirmed; they attend worship services; they celebrate the sacrament of the Lord's Supper; they are married in the church and buried in the church. Surely there is no shortage here of the Bread of Life! The bread of life, which is Jesus Christ, is something we simply take for granted in the so-called "Christian West."

But do not be deceived! If the true bread from heaven is going to produce eternal life, this bread must be received and appropriated. Bread must be taken and eaten!

"Whoever comes to me," Jesus said, "that person will never be hungry again."

"Whoever believes in me . . . that person will never thirst again."

"Whoever trusts in me . . . that person has eternal life."

Peter and the faithful disciples of Christ recognized this when they confessed: "Lord, to whom can we go? You have the words of eternal life. We have come to believe and know that you are the Holy One of God!" Anyone today who confesses Christ in this same way is someone who takes the bread of life seriously and who receives the life-giving power of that bread. Even so, there were people in those days of Peter and the other disciples who died in their sins because they did not believe in Jesus. They took offence at Jesus and the claims he proposed to make on their lives. They were not prepared to receive a gift from God, which called into question other gifts that they had received and in which they prided themselves. Jesus' radical call to discipleship and faith seemed too high a price to pay for bread—even for bread that produced eternal life. In Jesus' time there were many people who would have been happier simply to receive bread that sustained physical life for a day at a time. They were offended by the thought that there ought to be something more. This was a turning point in Jesus' ministry when some of the people who earlier had followed him zealously began to turn their backs on the Living Bread and return to their day-to-day existence.

Today also there are people, both near and far away, who have never tasted the bread of life—either because this bread has not been shared with them or because they refuse to eat. Jesus Christ is the Bread of Life. This Bread and this Life are precious gifts from the hand of God. But Bread of Life is an engaging gift. It must be received with thanksgiving and appropriated in faithful living.

Believing in Jesus involves staying with him, even when others take offence, turn their backs and abandon him. This is where true, eternal life begins. All who come to Jesus, believe in him, trust in him and confess him—those people will never be hungry again; they will never be thirsty again; they will never die, but will live forever!

9

Hard to Swallow
John 6:52-69

BEWARE OF counterfeit calamari! This was the warning, which rang out in the Südwest Rundfunk radio broadcast I was listening to some years back while driving through southern Germany. (For the uninitiated, 'calamari' is a Mediterranean delicacy—*squid*, which is normally sliced in rings, battered and deep-fried. If not prepared particularly well it can be rather tough and rubbery to chew!) I listened on to hear the testimony of a lady from Stuttgart who told about a holiday in Italy and how she had experienced first hand the danger of counterfeit calamari. She had chewed on a particular piece for thirty minutes before realizing that what she had in her mouth was not squid, but a piece of recycled automobile tires! Particularly suspect, according the broadcast, were sorts of calamari branded 'a'la Michelin' or 'a'la Firestone.' Up to this point, I was utterly shocked and amazed at what I was hearing on the news. Then I suddenly noted that the date of the broadcast was the first of April—April Fools Day! (Yes, this questionable holiday is observed internationally!) I quickly concluded that counterfeit calamari is a bit tough to chew and hard to swallow in more ways than one!

It was not a small number of disciples who passed a similar judgment upon the words that Jesus spoke in the synagogue in Capernaum (John 6:52-60). "This teaching is difficult," they said. "Who can accept it?" This word is 'tough to chew' and 'hard for us to swallow'! The hard word and the difficult saying had likewise to do with eating and drinking. Jesus was talking about eating flesh—*his* flesh; he was talking about drinking blood—*his* blood. "For my flesh is true food and my blood is true drink. Those who eat my flesh and drink my blood abide in me, and I in them. . . . Whoever eats me will live because of me."

This is indeed a hard word. This is not easy to 'chew' and even harder to 'swallow.' Actually, this word of Jesus is for many an unthinkable, an unspeakable word. What is more 'un-human' than to eat human flesh? What is more perverse to human nature than to drink human blood? For the Jewish disciples who heard Jesus speak these words in the synagogue, this was an *extremely hard teaching*. Even if they were somehow able to overcome their own human feelings of disgust and their own convictions of conscience concerning this matter, these people knew very well that their God had given them a commandment strictly prohibiting the abomination of eating human flesh.

Regarding the drinking of animal blood, God gave an explicit command to the Israelites in Leviticus 17:10-11. "If anyone of the house of Israel or of the aliens who reside among them eats any blood, I will set my face against that person who eats blood, and will cut that person off from the people. For the life of the flesh is in the blood; and I have given it to you for making atonement for your lives on the altar; for, as life, it is the blood that makes atonement."

Even if Jesus' teaching about eating his flesh and drinking his blood had been meant in a *figurative* sense, the idea would still have been distasteful at the least and abominable at the worst. (Indeed, there is no reason to believe that the disciples understood him to be speaking figuratively on this occasion!) "This teaching is difficult; who can accept it?"

But the teaching about eating flesh and drinking blood was not the only thing in Jesus' words that many of his followers found 'hard to swallow.' Jesus' portrayal of Israel's ancient history a bit earlier in this speech was, in itself, no tender morsel for those who were listening. Jesus suggested to the gathered crowd in the synagogue that there was bread from heaven, which surpassed their normal conception of bread from heaven. The distant ancestors of the people in Jesus' audience had eaten bread, which came to them directly from heaven, but they still died. Jesus suggested that the bread he would give them would procure eternal life.

Of course, Jesus' teaching about bread from heaven was referring to the time of the Israelites' wilderness wanderings after their exodus from Egypt. Moses had led the people into the desert where there was nothing to eat. God, however, provided for the people by sending them the manna. This was in itself an act of salvation and deliverance. The sending of this bread from heaven saved the lives of the multitudes of Israelites in the wilderness. But as Jesus recounted this history, he was making the point that there was better heavenly bread than the miraculous manna, which the forefathers ate in the desert. In contrast to this miraculous manna, there was a *true bread from heaven*. This true bread from heaven was Jesus himself.

"Very truly, I tell you, it was not Moses who gave you the bread from heaven, but it is my Father who gives you the true bread from Heaven" (6:32).

"I am the bread of life" (6:35a).

"Your ancestors ate manna in the wilderness, and they died" (6:49).

"I am the living bread that came down from heaven. Whoever eats of this bread will live for ever; and the bread that I will give for the life of the world is my flesh" (6:51).

To grasp and to accept the idea that Jesus was greater than Moses was no easy thing for the Jewish followers of Jesus. Indeed, they did anticipate in the course of their history the coming of a prophet *like Moses*. Moses himself had prophesied that God would raise up such a prophet *like him* from among the Israelites (Deuteronomy 18:15). The people were constantly on the lookout for this prophet *like Moses*, so that when John the Baptist came along the leaders of the people were eager to find out if he was *the prophet* (John 1:21). Some of the people in Jerusalem during the feast of tabernacles who heard Jesus' speaking in the temple courts were convinced that Jesus was *the prophet* (John 7:40). Even the Samaritan woman at the well had enough spiritual insight to perceive that Jesus was *a prophet* (John 4:19). There was no problem amongst the disciples or the leaders of the people to recognize Jesus as a prophet *like Moses*.

But, that Jesus was *greater than Moses*—this was a hard, difficult saying. Who could accept this notion? Who could possibly swallow this teaching, without choking on it? If Jesus had continued his ministry of feeding hungry people by miraculously multiplying loaves of bread, then there would have been no problem. This was acceptable; indeed, this was desirable. This was *like Moses* who provided manna for the Israelites in the desert. But the idea that Jesus should be the source of "living bread from heaven"—the kind of bread that people may eat and never die—this was too much. This notion that Jesus was *greater than Moses* was tough bread—impossible to chew up, swallow and digest.

In the final analysis, however, this word of Jesus about the bread of life was a hard teaching because it was unmistakably a word about the sacrificial death of God's Anointed One. At the beginning of chapter 6 of John's Gospel we learn that this discourse of Jesus in the Capernaum synagogue took place shortly before the Jewish Passover festival. This was the great annual feast in which thousands and thousands of sacrificial lambs were slaughtered at the Temple in Jerusalem in remembrance of the salvation of the entire nation, when God led the Israelites out of Egyptian captivity. It was a celebration of their new life and their new status as a people of God's own choosing. The bread of life discourse in this chapter is set carefully within the framework of this Passover Feast, in which Israel's history clearly showed how true life was gained through the sacrificial death of an innocent victim.

Jesus' own teaching in the Capernaum synagogue displays a direct reference to this historic and decisive event in the life of the people of Israel. "This living bread, this true bread from heaven, of which a person may eat and live forever—this bread is my flesh which I will offer as a sacrifice for the life of the world!" (It is interesting to note that, in the Greek text of John 6:51, the idea of 'giving on behalf of . . .' has distinct sacrificial overtones.) With these words Jesus was clearly signaling his own sacrificial death on the cross in the not-too-distant future. Jesus, the true Lamb of God who takes away the sins of the world, would very soon offer up his own life so that people who believe and trust in him would gain eternal life.

But this is no easy word. As simple as this gospel message may be, it is still very hard for many people to swallow—even for many religious people! This is a tough teaching for people who pride themselves in their own self-righteousness, for example. The word of the cross is a difficult word. Who can accept it? Who can take hold of this word and fully appreciated it without choking on the consequences? We are confronted with the word, which says that men and women need an innocent victim to suffer death on their behalf so that they can attain real life. Who can accept this? Who can accept a God who permits such an abomination?

The word of the cross of Jesus Christ is a hard word, a tough word, a difficult teaching. This word is 'stumbling block' and a word of 'foolishness' to many people in the world, both to the religious and to the non-religious alike (see 1 Corinthians 1:23). But this word about the cross of Christ, about the substitutional sacrifice of Jesus, is the word about true bread from heaven. It is the word of eternal life.

"Because of this many of his disciples turned back and no longer went about with him" (6:66). For many of the earlier disciples of Jesus this word about his sacrificial death was simply too tough to chew, too hard to swallow. They could not and would not accept it.

This is the history of the word of Jesus down to today. When it comes to the matter of Christ's death on the cross as a sacrifice for the life of the world, many people simply cannot or will not listen. When I was pastor of the Christliche Gemeinde in Tübingen, Germany I received a letter from a young man who lived in the north of the country. In his letter he posed a number of questions dealing with the Christian faith, interested in hearing the opinion and response of an American theologian. The author of the letter did indeed consider himself to be a Christian, and I have no doubt that he was. But precisely the word of the cross—this word of the sacrificial death of Jesus Christ—was too strange for his ears.

This word, so he maintained, belonged to an ancient conception of the world, which was no longer tenable at the end of the twentieth century. (That is, it belonged to the world of the Old Testament and ancient Judaism!) Moreover, he felt that this word of the cross was simply not compatible with the 'Jesus' of his own experience. It was a word that was stamped not by the person of the historical Jesus, but by the worldview of the early Church.

The opinion of this young German is really not so very rare today. Many of the popular books about Jesus on best-seller lists and on bookstore shelves today take this same view. People seem to want to know something *new* about Jesus, other than the words that they have heard from the pages of scripture. They want some new revelation from the ancient writings of Qumran or from other hidden, esoteric texts that portray a more palatable Jesus for today's society. Even down to today the word of the cross is a stumbling block for some and it is sheer folly to others.

What is the essential difference between people who take offence at this hard word of Jesus and those who recognize in it the wisdom and power of God? It really has to do with how these people evaluate themselves in the first place, how they view their own status before God. Men and women who, because of pride and self-righteousness, are unable to admit their own sin before God or who count their own personal sin as negligible will likely find a word about the cross of Christ highly unappetizing. They will not want to hear about a Jesus who took sin so seriously that he was willing to sacrifice himself for this sin.

On the other hand, anyone who recognizes his or her own guilt before God and who understands that there is no human way out of the predicament which sin precipitates is ready to receive the word of the cross of Christ as true gospel. This is the person who is fed up with the vicious cycle of sin and self-righteousness. For those who are experiencing God's salvation, the word of Christ is not a hard, tough word, which is impossible to receive and appropriate. Rather, it is a word full of God's power and God's wisdom.

Faith is the very thing that is able to transform the tough word about the cross of Jesus Christ into the tender, welcome word of salvation. More precisely, it is a trusting, faithful commitment that is able to bring about the transformation. That is, full trust and complete, unwavering commitment to Jesus Christ is required. He alone is able to offer men and women the bread of life, for he alone *is* the true bread of life. Faith involves complete trust in the 'Jesus' whose promise ultimately has to do with life. "It is the spirit that gives life; the flesh is useless. The words that I have spoken to you are spirit and life" (6:63). Ultimately, this word of Jesus is not only a word about the abomination of the cross and of death, but it is a word of life. It is a word of glory, of hope and of resurrection from the dead (see 6:54, 62).

It is through faith, through trusting in Jesus Christ, that we eat his flesh and we drink his blood. It is through faith, through trusting in Jesus Christ, that we receive the true, living bread from heaven, which causes us to live forever. It is through faith, through trusting in Jesus Christ, that we hear the word of his sacrificial death—a word that speaks to us at the same time of our own desperate human situation under the reign of sin. It is through faith, through trusting in Jesus Christ, that we share the hope of eternal life, the hope of resurrection from the dead. This is what it means to believe in Jesus.

Jesus knew that there were some followers who did not believe in him and who did not trust him in this way. He realized that there were some disciples who took offence at him because they found his words to be too tough, too hard and too unacceptable. As Jesus noticed that some were leaving him, he turned to the twelve who constituted the inner circle of his band of followers and asked if they too wanted to go away. This same question Jesus constantly puts to us, his modern-day disciples as we are confronted time and time again with the 'hard' words of the gospel. Will we also turn away from him when the word seems too hard, when it seems to demand too much or when the commitment of discipleship seems more than we can bear?

Believing in Jesus is an ongoing commitment of trust in him and faithfulness to his word. Let us learn to respond to Jesus' question in the same way that Peter and the other eleven disciples did on that occasion: "Lord, to whom can we go? You have the words of eternal life. We have come to believe and know that you are the Holy One of God!" (John 6:68-69).

10

Thieves and Bandits
John 10:1-10

THIEVES AND bandits are clever, sly people. Indeed, they must be clever and sly if they are going to accomplish their goals of stealing, killing and destroying. No one expects thieves and bandits to be open and honest about their business affairs. No one anticipates that they will go about their perverse activities in a straightforward, transparent fashion. Honesty and forthrightness are not the qualities they display. On the contrary, as one would naturally expect, thieves and bandits go about their business in a crooked manner. They loiter about in the dark shadows. They lie and deceive. They wait for that opportune moment when the target victim is completely unsuspecting and most vulnerable. They employ the lowest, dirtiest tricks and maneuvers. They see to it that their victims have less in life to enjoy.

Each time a bandit or thief strikes, the story is painfully familiar, yet startlingly unreal. A telephone call comes late in the night: "Hello, Mr. and Mrs. Dietrich. This is Robert, a friend of your son Jochen. Jochen was badly injured in an automobile accident tonight just outside the disco and was taken to the trauma center in Tübingen."

The parents quickly get dressed and rush to the hospital. But no one at the hospital knows anything about their son or about any automobile accident. The parents drive on to the scene of the supposed accident. Again they do not find their son, nor does anyone at the disco know anything about an accident. All of a sudden the penny drops! The parents then telephone their next-door neighbors asking them to hurry to see about their house, left empty and unprotected. But it is too late. The break-in has already occurred and the house has been ransacked. This is the way that thieves and bandits operate.

"Very truly, I tell you," says Jesus, "anyone who does not enter the sheepfold by the gate but climbs in by another way is a thief and a bandit." Even the church of Jesus Christ is not exempt from the danger of hostile break-in by thieves and bandits. This is the very danger of which Jesus warns his disciples in John 10. There were, there are and there will be people who move about under the cover of shadows and darkness trying craftily to infiltrate the church. They seek access over the wall, through the 'back door', but not at all through the main gate, which is Jesus Christ.

Some of these are relatively easy to identify. For example, it is fairly easy to point a finger at those persons and groups that worship a strange god, or even no god. There are certain well-known 'Christian sects,' which are fairly transparent. But these are not the ones that Jesus is warning his disciples about in this passage—at least not in the first instance. Much more wily and deceitful, much more dangerous are those people and groups who maintain that they belong to the Church, but who craftily bypass the gate to the sheepfold.

This parable of Jesus about the good shepherd and the gate to the sheepfold appears in the text of John's gospel sandwiched between the narratives of two instances where Jesus has been rejected as God's representative and as God's Son. This outright rejection of Jesus has come from persons who themselves represented the mainline position of Jesus' own religious community.

Immediately prior to this encounter Jesus had healed a man who had been born blind. For the first time in his life this unfortunate man was able to see. The religious leaders, however, were furious. They did not want to believe that Jesus had healed the man. They wanted to disprove the whole incident as one big hoax, avoiding the logical conclusion that Jesus was acting with the full authority of God. Although the personal testimony of the man who had been born blind was straightforward, they refused to believe him. They tried to make him out to be a liar. They cross-examined his parents, whose simple testimony confirmed that this man was their son and that he had been born blind. More than this they would not say because they were afraid of the religious leaders. In the end the man who had been healed was excommunicated from the synagogue because he maintained that his healer was acting in the power and under the authority of God. Otherwise how could he have opened the eyes of someone born blind? Jesus concluded from this whole incident that the ones who were truly blind were the very leaders themselves. Though they maintained that they could clearly see what God was doing in the world, they stumbled over the activity and presence of God in the ministry of Jesus. This was a more serious blindness than the blindness that had afflicted the simple peasant man.

Immediately following Jesus' parable of the shepherd and sheep in the text of John's gospel (John 10:22-39), we find a further incident in the Jerusalem temple. Here Jesus boldly proclaims to be acting in the name and under the direct authority of God: "The Father and I are one!" The reaction of the religious leaders on this occasion was a violent one. They picked up stones, ready to stone Jesus to death, because he was claiming divine authority in this way. They tried to arrest him and to incite a lynch mob, but Jesus was able to escape from their hands.

The religious leaders were unwilling to entertain the possibility that Jesus was the Messiah, the Son of God. There must be some other gate into the Kingdom of God! There must be some more suitable, acceptable way to get into God's sheepfold. There must be another, more accessible door. Perhaps there are *many* other doors, which lead to eternal life in God's presence. Surely, Jesus could not be the *only* way. This exclusivity he was claiming under the authority of God, as the Son of God, was offensive to the audience of religious leaders who felt that they had direct access to all the necessary doors into God's kingdom—and this quite apart from the person of Jesus of Nazareth!

Can we today really imagine that God's Kingdom remains closed to some people simply because they take offence at the notion that Jesus is the Christ, the Son of God? Can we, in good conscience, maintain that there are people who exclude themselves from the riches of God's Kingdom simply because they stumble over Jesus? Is it essential to believe in a 'Jesus' who offers up his life on a Roman cross, and who three days after this cruel torture is raised from the dead? Is it not sufficient when men and women simply attempt to conduct their lives in an orderly way and, insofar as they are personally gifted, to do good deeds? Is it not sufficient, when men and women simply believe that there is a God and attempt to honor this God in their own hearts insofar as they are personally able?

Is it ultimately so terribly important for people to buy into this Jesus—a shepherd who models redemptive sacrifice and expects no less of his flock? Many people to-day are strongly inclined to say: "No. It is not ultimately important that men and women believe specifically in Jesus." Even many *Christians and church leaders* today are happy to concede that it is sufficient when others simply have the desire to honor God in whatever way they feel most comfortable, whether or not they choose to believe specifically in Jesus. It is enough, they say, when people simply try to love their neighbors, to make peace, to en-gage themselves in environmental protection activities, to seek justice for oppressed and to demonstrate their oppo-sition to war. Indeed, these are the very things that Jesus emphasized in his own teachings. Therefore, when the people of the world do these kinds of things, does it really matter whether they believe specifically in Jesus?

But Jesus' voice commands a higher place of author-ity than the voices of strangers. "I am the gate for the sheep", he insists. "*I am the gate.* Whoever enters by me will be saved, and will come in and go out and find pas-ture." Jesus is the gate to the sheepfold. Jesus provides the way into the kingdom of God. Jesus is the door to eter-nal life. Those who insist upon finding other gates and ways and doors are, in Jesus' words, thieves and bandits. Believing in Jesus means accepting him as the true shep-herd of God's flock and trusting his voice over against the sometimes-enticing voices of strangers.

11

An Anointing in Bethany
John 12:1-8

DIFFERENT PEOPLE behave in very different ways, even in the context of the same social setting. Anyone who has ever attended a wedding reception and observed the behavior of the various and sundry guests will know exactly what I mean. This is especially evident in instances where the bride and groom come from very different families, social backgrounds and perhaps even national and cultural backgrounds. What seems proper behavior to the one might seem very inappropriate, perhaps extremely offensive to the next person. People are highly individual and tend to react in different ways to the same set of circumstances.

How would we have behaved if we had been in Bethany on that day and invited to sit at the dinner table with Jesus and his friends? Perhaps one person might behave extremely self-consciously, exercising the kind of politeness with which one might greet a member of the royal family. Another might react very informally (the American way!) with a shake of the hand and a slap on the back for Jesus. Some might prefer to cower away in the corner, behind the other people, out of shyness or feelings of guilt and inadequacy. Still others might rush to Jesus with hearts full of joy and surround him with a big hug.

Mary, the sister of Lazarus and Martha, greeted Jesus by taking a bottle of very expensive perfume made from pure nard oil, pouring it over Jesus' feet and drying it off with her hair.

Does this not seem rather unusual behavior in this sort of social setting? Why did Mary react in this way to Jesus' presence? No one else reacted to Jesus in this way. Indeed there were a number of other *appropriate* options for honoring Jesus on this occasion.

For example, there was the option which Martha, Mary's sister, chose. The occasion of this gathering with Jesus was a great banquet in his honor. Martha was helping to serve the guests at the table. This was, of course, typical behavior for Martha! Luke's gospel relates a story about another occasion when Jesus was a dinner guest in the home of Mary and Martha (Luke 10:38-42). This time also Martha was the one who was busy with meal preparation and serving, while Mary sat at Jesus' feet and listened to him talk. When Martha became upset with her sister for not helping out with the *women's* work, Jesus gently set the matter straight: "Martha, Martha, you are concerned and troubled about so many things; but only one thing is necessary. Your sister has made the better choice, and it will not be taken away from her!"

Martha was just like my mother! For as long as I can remember, whenever we entertained the minister's family in our home, my mother always had so much nervous energy that she simply could not sit still long enough to enjoy the meal herself. She was always up and down from the table, back and forth into the kitchen, seeing about something, getting something else that she had forgotten; and then, at some point during the meal, my father would notice what was going on and would insist: "Esther, sit down and eat!" She would then sit down and begin to enjoy the meal herself for two or three minutes. But then she would soon start again with getting up and down and going here and there in order to fetch and serve. For when there is a special meal going on and guests at the table, *someone* has to serve. This service is indeed a way of honoring the guests, particularly the guest of honor. That which was typical 'Martha' and typical 'Esther' could have been an example for Mary as well. She could have honored Jesus at this meal by being a behind-the-scenes servant.

Alternatively, Mary could have followed the example of her brother Lazarus on this occasion. Lazarus was honoring Jesus by participating in the fellowship around the table with Jesus and the other guests. He was simply enjoying the festive banquet. Most likely, Mary would have been sharply criticized if she had acted in this way since it would have been highly uncustomary for a woman to sit at a banquet table with men. But it would not have been out of character for Mary to behave in an uncustomary way. Again, we are reminded of that same story in Luke's gospel where Mary sat at Jesus' feet along with the other disciples and listened to him talk rather than resigning herself to 'the women's place' in the kitchen with her sister Martha. We are reminded again that Jesus commended her for choosing the better option. Could she not have honored Jesus in the same way on this occasion by simply enjoying the table fellowship together with the other guests?

Mary could even have honored Jesus on this occasion by following the advice of Judas Iscariot. She could have sold her bottle of expensive perfume for the amount of money earned by a typical day-laborer for a whole year of work. Just think how far that much money would go in terms of charity work, or supporting the itinerant ministry of Jesus and his disciples. John's gospel tells us that this event took place at the time just prior to the Passover Feast. It was common practice during this feast time for people to make charitable contributions to the poor, in much the same way that we today make special contributions to charitable organizations at Christmas time. This was seen as a way of honoring God in response to His goodness. John tells us that Judas' real motivation in making this suggestion was not because he cared about the poor, but because he was in charge of dispensing the common funds and he had a habit of lining his own pockets from the common purse. But his suggestion was not a bad one. Giving to the poor is a good thing. It is pleasing and honoring to God. Indeed it is something that God requires. To mark the special significance of this banquet occasion, Mary could have sold her bottle of expensive perfume and honored Jesus by giving the money to poor people.

But Mary did not follow the advice of Judas; she did not follow the example of her brother Lazarus; and she did not follow the lead of her sister Martha. She took her bottle of expensive, pure nard oil, poured it over Jesus' feet and dried his feet with her hair.

What motivated Mary to behave in this highly peculiar way on this occasion, when there were so many other, *normal* possibilities of showing honor to Jesus? Jesus explained to the other guests that Mary had saved this expensive perfumed oil to anoint him for the day of his burial. The poor would always be around and there would always be plentiful opportunities for everyone, each in his or her own way, to make appropriate charitable contributions. But this was a special service, a special honor, which only Mary was in a position to perform for Jesus at this particular point in time.

Are we to imagine, however, that Mary had any idea that this 'day of Jesus' burial' was so near? Did she actually believe that there would ever come such a day for Jesus—this man who just recently had raised her own brother Lazarus from the dead? Did Mary realize when performing this honor that she was anointing Jesus' body for the day of his death? If so, why was it just his feet that she anointed, and not his whole body? Why did she mop it up with her hair? There are many *why's* in this story!

I think the probable explanation to all these *why's* is connected more with Mary's own life and personal needs than it is with Jesus' need to have his body anointed with oil for burial. The story of what Mary did on this occasion is truly remarkable, when one stops to think about it. On the one hand, it was indeed customary for the host at a dinner party to pour olive oil over the heads of the honored guests. A good example of this is Psalm 23:5 where the psalmist rejoices over his special treatment as the guest of honor when seated at a table with his enemies present. This honor is shown when the host of the banquet anoints his head with oil. Furthermore, it was expected at a banquet of this nature that the host—or, more likely, the house servants—would wash the feet of the guests of honor upon their arrival. For their feet would be dusty and dirty—likely even muddy and smelly. Who knows what kind of filth they had to walk through in the public streets! These streets, of course, were not necessarily paved and they served as passages not only for people, but also for herds of animals. The streets were also used as receptacles for rubbish and refuse from homes and shops along the way! Thus, the washing of feet at a banquet meal was more than just a nicety; it was a hygienic necessity.

The fact, however, that Mary poured her expensive perfumed oil on Jesus' dirty feet, and that she mopped up and dried this muddy, dirty, oily mess with her own hair—does this behavior not seem a bit 'over the top'? How improper and inappropriate of Mary in the presence of one so great as Jesus! How *common* and *unsophisticated!* How *messy* and *revolting!* What could be more *humiliating* than what Mary did in this story? What could have been more *self-debasing?*

But this is precisely the point! Mary could have busied herself along with her sister in serving tables at the banquet. There was indeed much work to do and somebody had to do it. After all, this banquet was given in Jesus' honor.

Likewise, Mary could have sat at the table with Jesus along with her brother Lazarus. That would have been a very comfortable, enjoyable experience. It is, after all, impolite to stand on and watch while other people are eating!

Or Mary could have devoted her attention to social action in the name of Jesus. She could have used her resources for charity and brought honor to Jesus in this way. There would have been a lot of good that she could accomplish with the sum of money obtained from the sale of the perfume.

But more important for Mary than all these other possibilities to do good things was her own personal need to bow before Jesus in humble, selfless submission. Why was it necessary for Mary to humble herself in this way before Jesus, in this act of utter self-denial and self-sacrifice? It was necessary because Mary was guilty of sin; and she knew it! The parallel account of this story in Luke's gospel (7:36—8:3) indicates just what kind of a sinner this woman was (though Luke in this instance does not mention Mary by name). According to Luke's account this woman had a 'certain reputation' in the village; that is, she was a prostitute. Everyone knew this about her, and no self-respecting, upright person in the village would dare to have any kind of contact with this sort of woman.

Luke's account of the story also mentions that, in addition to the nard oil, this woman used her tears to wash the feet of Jesus. There can be no doubt whatsoever that this self-debasing act of a sinful woman is a clear sign of her conversion and her faith in Jesus Christ. It shows her remorse. It indicates repentance, dying to oneself, turning away from the old way of life, and turning towards the one to whose feet she was clinging. This is the first and the decisive step in a life of faith in Jesus Christ.

Luke tells us also that Jesus forgave her sins. Her faith in Jesus Christ brought her salvation on that day. "Leave her alone," Jesus said to the other guests who were quick to criticize her actions. "This woman has made the right choice and has displayed the appropriate behavior. This woman knows who I am. She knows what I have come to do. She understands the meaning of my imminent death, burial and resurrection. Everywhere in the world, wherever the gospel is proclaimed, it will also be reported about this woman and what she has done. People will remember this act of hers! So, leave her alone; she has chosen the better option and it will not be taken away from her!"

There are times when we really must get to work and busy ourselves with various services that we have to perform in the church and in our daily lives, in order to bring honor to Jesus. There is much work to be done in order that the Church of Christ is served and helped and built up. On those occasions Martha's example is a good one for us to follow. We need to roll up our sleeves and get to work!

There are other times when we really need to relax and simply enjoy the table fellowship with Jesus and the other disciples who are gathered together. Our fellowship times in worship and on other occasions should be times of refreshing, when we can simply sit back and drink in the blessing of this wonderful fellowship. At such times we should remember Lazarus in this story and remember that we can honor Jesus by following his example.

Indeed, there are times when we should follow even the advice of Judas, the betrayer. There are occasions when we should make major contributions to aid the poor and the socially disadvantaged. Christians do have social responsibilities, and Judas' advice about giving to the poor is good advice, even though he himself was a thief and a hypocrite.

But there are also times when Mary's example is the one we need to follow, and no one of us is exempt. There are times when we need to empty ourselves and bow humbly at Jesus' feet; when we need to confess our sins to him openly and remorsefully; when we need consciously to turn away from those sins and throw ourselves completely upon Jesus Christ. For each of us, just like Mary, has that same need to hear the words of Jesus to us: "Your sins are forgiven! Your faith has saved you! Go in peace!"

12

Who May See Jesus?
John 12:20-36

WHO SHOULD be permitted to come to Jesus? In theory there is really no question at all in this matter. *Everyone* is allowed access to Jesus. No one is excluded from coming to Jesus, regardless of who she or he is or is not! "Look, the *whole world* has gone after him!" complained the pious religious leaders in John 12:19. "And I, when I am lifted up from the earth," proclaimed Jesus "will draw *all people* to myself" (12:32). This principle is borne out time and time again in the history of the church, and particularly from the very outset of the Pentecost event. Joel had prophesied that God would pour out his Spirit upon *all flesh* (Acts 2:17ff). The Apostle Peter, who was himself a Jew, came to understand through the conversion of the Gentile centurion Cornelius that "God shows no partiality, but in every nation anyone who fears him and does what is right is acceptable to him" (Acts 10:34-35). The examples could go on and on. We live in a time when many church groups are trying to be more 'seeker sensitive' with regard to people who wish to encounter Jesus. The Church has always affirmed the principle that *every human being is permitted to come to Jesus.*

But sometimes theory and practice are two quite distinct things. What we agree to on paper does not always work out in the laboratory of life. So it was, when some 'Greeks' who were present for the Passover celebration in Jerusalem came seeking an audience with Jesus, it was not immediately clear to the disciples Philip and Andrew what the proper procedure was. They knew, for example, that Jesus was extremely busy at this time. A quick look at the situation would have indicated to anyone that Jesus' appointment diary was fully booked. This was the last week of his life. There was a lot going on. Just the Passover feast itself was full of activity and excitement and preparations. It was not a good time for scheduling extra meetings.

Jesus himself was constantly on the go during this time. Only a short time earlier Jesus had raised Lazarus from the dead in the nearby village of Bethany. He was in great demand with "the whole world running after him" as we noted above. There were so many people who wanted an audience with Jesus at this particular time. There were *too many* people who wanted to see Jesus. There literally were not enough hours in the day for everyone to see Jesus who wanted to spend time with him. It was physically impossible.

But this was really no new development in the final days of Jesus' life. This was the situation throughout his entire public ministry. There were constantly men and women and children flocking to him, to see him, touch him, hear him, speak with him, and eat with him. During the three years of his public ministry Jesus seldom had time for himself. He had little time to eat, to sleep, to rest, or even to pray. Often he simply had to go without some of these essentials.

We might well imagine, this being the case, that Jesus often had too little time for his own disciples. They had questions of him that went unanswered, problems that went unsolved, fears and anxieties that went uncomforted, because there simply was not time enough for Jesus to deal with their needs. For this reason we see that the disciples themselves were often struggling with this practical question of who should be permitted to see Jesus. They were the ones on the firing line. People continually came to the disciples looking for an introduction to Jesus. Whom should they allow to see Jesus and whom should they turn away? What about children who were being brought by their mothers for Jesus to lay hands on them and confer a blessing? What about a sinful tax collector, like Zacchaeus, who was so short that he had to climb a tree to get a glance at Jesus over the heads of the crowd? What about ten outcast men (one of whom was a foreigner and hence, a double outcast) who, because of their dreadful skin disease were not allowed contact with 'normal' people? What about a prostitute who wanted to anoint the feet of Jesus with expensive perfume? What about a blind beggar at the side of the road? What about Mary, whose sister felt that she should be helping with the meal preparations rather than sitting at Jesus' feet and listening to his teachings?

Presently, in a week full of 'busyness,' excitement, uncertainty and fear, came another request to the disciple Philip: "Sir, we wish to see Jesus." This time it was a group of Greeks who were seeking an introduction to Jesus. John's gospel indicates that these Greeks were in Jerusalem to participate in the worship at the Passover festival; thus they must have had some connection with or leanings toward the Jewish religion. But it is equally clear from the way they are presented in John's gospel that these individuals were foreigners. They were in Jerusalem only as visitors. It is questionable whether they even spoke the 'proper' language of Palestine. They stuck out from the normal worshippers at the temple, as foreigners often do stand out in a crowd. These 'seekers' were outsiders, as far as Philip and the other disciples were concerned. What to do? Philip went to Andrew for counsel, and both of them went on to discuss the matter with Jesus personally. How should they respond to the request of these outsiders who were asking for some of Jesus' precious time?

The answer, however, which Jesus gave to Philip and Andrew, is really quite remarkable. "The hour has come," he replied, "for the Son of Man to be glorified. Very truly, I tell you, unless a grain of wheat falls into the earth and dies, it remains just a single grain; but if it dies, it bears much fruit" (12:24).

Philip and Andrew had come to Jesus with a simple question as to whether he had time and energy enough to meet with a group of Greek-speaking people. Then, out of the blue, Jesus began this speech about 'glory,' about seeds being planted and growing, about *dying*. What did all this have to do with the situation at hand? Had Jesus misunderstood the question? Was he so pre-occupied that he did not grasp the nature of the request? Was he simply ignoring the situation at hand? Or was Jesus trying to point these disciples and perhaps also the group of seekers to a deeper, more significant issue?

Upon reflection, what is there actually to *see* when someone comes to Jesus? Who is it that people want to become acquainted with when they seek an audience with him? Is it simply a matter of meeting just one more person, one more human being? Is it just a matter of having contact with a great 'personality,' a 'super-star'?

Not at all! There is much more than this! The hour has come! The glory of the Son of Man is about to become apparent! It is the glory of God himself! The more significant question in this story is who may be permitted to lay eyes on the glory of God. "Who shall ascend the hill of the Lord?" asks the psalmist in Psalm 24:3. "And who shall stand in his holy place?" We know from the Old Testament that very few individuals in the history of God's people were actually allowed to see God's glory. Even Moses was not allowed to view the complete glory of God, for fear of death (Exodus 33:12-33). The prophet Isaiah, however, recounts a personal experience in the Jerusalem temple when he caught a vision of the heavenly throne of God. The house of the Lord was filled with smoke and he heard the heavenly beings proclaiming that the "whole earth is full of his glory" (Isaiah 6:3). Jesus explains a little further on in John's gospel (John 12:41) that it was his own glory that Isaiah had seen in his vision in the temple. This is an extremely important point to be made in the context of a passage of scripture where there are foreigners who come seeking an audience with Jesus.

Even in the gospel accounts of the New Testament we find very few people who, during the ministry of Jesus, are allowed to catch a glimpse of the full glory of Christ. Only three members of the inner circle of the twelve disciples—Peter, James and John—were allowed to ascend the mountain with Jesus and experience his glorious transfiguration. Philip and Andrew were themselves outsiders and out of their depth when the Greeks came with their request to see Jesus. Who were *they* to make a decision about who may or may not be permitted to see Jesus' glory? When it came to the question of the glory of the Son of Man, Philip and Andrew were as much strangers as these Greek foreigners in Jerusalem were.

Likewise, who are we today to make decisions about who may or may not be introduced to Jesus and to his glory? Who are we, to say to people today 'yes' or 'no,'

'you may come or go'? Can we make such weighty judg-
ments simply on the basis of a woman's nationality; on
the basis of a man's first language; on the basis of people's
customs or political persuasions; on the basis of their
clothes or the color of their skin or on the basis of their
personal problems and their sins? Are we in a position to
make these kinds of decisions? We are just as much strangers and foreigners to the glory of God as the others who
appear strange and foreign to us. "For there is no distinc-
tion, since all have sinned and fall short of the glory of
God" (Romans 3:22-23). Who can be permitted to see
the glory of God in Jesus Christ? Everyone is a stranger
and foreigner in this matter.

Still, there is a possibility for us, and for all, to come
to Jesus and to look upon his glory. This is actually the
point of Jesus' curious reply to Philip and Andrew when
they came bringing the request of the Greeks: "Those who
love their life lose it, and those who hate their life in this
world will keep it for eternal life. Whoever serves me must
follow me, and where I am, there will my servant be also.
Whoever serves me, the Father will honor. Now my soul
is troubled. And what should I say—'Father, save me from
this hour'? No, it is for this reason that I have come to this
hour. Father, glorify your name. . . . Now is the judgment
of this world; now the ruler of this world will be driven
out. And I, when I am lifted up from the earth, will draw
all people to myself" (John 12:25-28, 31-33).

In these verses Jesus shows his disciples that the
question which we have been considering all along—
the question about who may be permitted to see Jesus
in his glory—is the wrong question altogether. The
principle, which we know deep in our hearts, is true. Every
man, woman and child is welcome to come to Jesus. But
whether this principle is put into practice depends upon

each individual person. The most important question for us is not the question that we ask (that is, the question about who should be permitted to see Jesus). The most important question is the one, which Jesus himself asks of each person who desires to come and see him; that is, *Who is prepared to follow Jesus in his very footsteps?*

What Jesus requires of his disciples in this passage has a direct reference to the pathway his footsteps took in this final week of his life. Jesus' pathway involves giving up the life of this world; it is a pathway of doing the will of the Father; it is a pathway of suffering and even death. But also Jesus' pathway leads to resurrection from the dead, to new life, to glory. It brings about the transformation of the old into something gloriously new in the presence of God. The question that Jesus asks is a *faith question*. Believing in Jesus is a matter of following faithfully in his footsteps.

A kernel of wheat is, in itself, nothing terribly special. But when it is buried in the earth—when it dies—only then can it be transformed into a beautiful, tall, fruit-bearing and life-giving plant. It is sown in its simplicity; but it is transformed into a glorious new reality. This is the pathway to glory that Jesus has opened up for all people, the pathway to life eternal. The important question, however, is this: Who is prepared to believe in Jesus in this way? Who is prepared to make a commitment to following in the footsteps of Jesus in the final week of his life? Who is prepared to lose the life of this world in order to gain new life with Jesus? Who is prepared to die to sin in order to live to God in Christ Jesus? Who is ready to be united with Christ in his death, to be buried with him in baptism in order to share his own new life and in his God-given glory through the power of the Holy Spirit?

"Sir, we wish to see Jesus." It is a simple request, a noble desire. Down to this very day there are still people who seek Jesus in this simple, humble way. I am one such person and I dare say that most of the readers of this book will find this same simple request constantly surfacing and resurfacing in their own hearts. It is really only natural that people are constantly looking for a clearer picture and a closer encounter with Jesus Christ. Jesus himself prophesied that when he was lifted up from the earth on the cross he would draw to himself *all people:* Greeks, Jews, Muslims, Hindus, Buddhists, Americans, Europeans, Asians, Africans, men, women, red-skinned, white-skinned, black-skinned, yellow-skinned, blue-collar, white-collar, blind, lame, healthy, sick, rich, poor, high, low, mighty, weak. It does not matter. Jesus promises to draw *all people* to himself. There are plenty of spaces in Jesus' appointment diary. The question is not who may come to Jesus, but rather, *who will follow Jesus!*

13

Living in Faith
John 14:1-7

BELIEVING IN Jesus does not guarantee that everything in the life of a Christian will be always, only happy, fortunate and peaceful. Believing in Jesus does not guarantee that Christians, simply by virtue of the fact that they are Christians, will never experience those troughs of life's existence when they feel alone and forgotten. They are not exempt from moments when they feel disappointed and frustrated; when they feel exhausted and drained of energy; when they feel afraid, insecure, terrified, orphaned and abandoned by the God in whom they put their trust.

Many are the modern preachers of prosperity and many are their disciples who maintain that the Christian life is heaven on earth. As long as you *believe in Jesus* then your life will be a bed of roses—no sorrows, no fears, no disappointments, no problems—only joy and peace and smiling faces and friendly words and loving deeds! Faith in Christ, they say, is like a magical key, which opens up the door to the good life!

This prosperity gospel is not new. Already in Jesus' own time there were those who held this magical, mystical view of faith in God. The Jewish philosopher Philo of Alexandria maintained that "Faith in God is the only true and certain thing, for it holds the comfort of life, the fulfillment of good hopes, the absence of all evil and the fullness of goodness, . . . the possession of happiness" (Philo, *On the Life of Abraham* 268). What a lovely picture of the life of faith in God! Who would not want this kind of life? Who would ever hesitate one second to become a Christian? All the church buildings in the world would be bursting at the seams with men and women who were seeking precisely this life of pure bliss. Evangelism would be as easy as "A, B, C" if the message that we had to preach was: "Only believe in Jesus and every desire of your life will be instantly fulfilled!"

But when all is said and done, the person who believes in Jesus is still a human being. Even the believer experiences the troughs of life, which time and time again confront all people. So it is that Christian women and men and children become weary, weak, and disheartened. Thinking at times that their heavenly Father has abandoned them as orphans, they feel alone, fearful, insecure, perhaps even terrified. This is the picture of Jesus' disciples, which we see in John 14.

The disciples certainly displayed a living faith in Jesus. They had stuck beside him through thick and thin. They recognized him to be the savior of the world. But they were weary. So much was going on around them in so little time, they scarce could take it all in. Lazarus had been raised from the dead. Jesus had faced a very hostile reception by the religious leaders in Jerusalem. There were all the busy preparations for the celebration of the Passover Feast, now looming before them. In the midst of all this, there was an unending stream of people hovering about, pushing their way to the front, to catch a glimpse of Jesus and to have a word with him. The disciples were exhausted and suffering from burnout along with the emotional depression that accompanies this kind of exhaustion.

Moreover, the disciples were disappointed in many of their hopes for Jesus. The moment of truth was upon them. It was the time when Jesus really ought to be showing his hand, both for the sake of his followers and for the shame of his adversaries. Jesus ought to be making preparations for a public display of his divine authority as the Messiah of Israel. He ought to be preparing his strategy for crushing his enemies and presenting himself as the mighty King of Israel. Instead, he was speaking to them about his imminent suffering and death on a Roman cross. The disciples were bitterly disappointed. Where did this leave them?

The disciples felt themselves alone and abandoned and with nowhere to turn. Jesus had spoken to them on a number of occasions about his departure from them. He had indicated that they would not be able to go with him. They felt afraid and insecure; the rug had been pulled out from underneath their feet. The future looked bleak under the present circumstances. They were disappointed, alone, afraid and very, very weary. They were feeling all these emotions *in spite of* their faith in Jesus Christ.

It is normal for people, when faced with one of life's deep, dark moments, to ask themselves whether it is really worth it to believe in God. Does faith really make any difference in life? Is there any advantage to being a Christian? Is there any sense in it? As 'unchristian' as these thoughts may seem, I would suggest that they are still fairly normal even for Christians when they face life's dark moments. I am fairly certain that this is what Jesus' disciples themselves were feeling that last week with Jesus in Jerusalem. This is the context in which Jesus' own words of comfort find their best interpretation.

Jesus said to his weary, disappointed and fearful disciples: "Do not let your hearts be troubled. *Believe in God, believe also in me!*" Faith in Jesus is not in vain. Believing in Jesus does indeed make a major difference in the life of a man or woman. The future may seem hopeless when we are caught in the depths of a dark moment. We may feel helpless in those circumstances when it appears that we are abandoned and alone. But even at those times there is still a word of comfort, a word of hope. Comfort and hope are rooted in our believing in Jesus, in our standing firm in our trust in God.

Comfort and the hope appear in Jesus' own words as he promises us that our faith is not in vain. In the depths of the deepest trough of life, believing in Jesus makes all the difference in the world. Believing in Jesus makes the difference between life and death! As Jesus' disciples found themselves in the depths of despair, they did not even want to think about the possibilities of a future. The future, which they had imagined for themselves and for their Lord, was now firmly out of the picture, and they felt that there was no acceptable alternative. There was no other future that they wished to entertain. But Jesus' words of comfort in this dark time were words about the future, about a future that they could not yet imagine. "For those who trust in me," Jesus was telling them, "there is *indeed* a future—the brightest future of all!" "In my Father's house there are many dwelling places. If it were not so, would I have told you that I go to prepare a place for you? And if I go and prepare a place for you, I will come again and will take you to myself, so that where I am, there you may be also. . . . I will not leave you orphaned; I am coming to you" (John 14:2-3; 18).

What difference does it make for someone facing the darkness of a helpless present and a hopeless future to believe in Jesus? It makes this difference: In the midst of hopelessness she or he has hope—namely, the promise of Jesus who says he is preparing a place for that person. It is the promise of a future with God! But this is not the only difference which believing in Jesus can make in the life of a disciple who is facing a dark present and an uncertain future. There is also something more immediate. Jesus' physical absence from his disciples does not mean, as his disciples feared, that they were to be abandoned as helpless orphans in a hostile world. Quite the opposite, Jesus' presence with the Father would mean that these disciples would receive in bountiful measure all the help, power, strength, comfort and even glory, which they would need for their lives on earth. "The one who believes in me," Jesus assured them, "will also do the works that I do and, in fact, will do greater works than these, *because I am going to the Father*. I will do whatever you ask in my name, so that the Father may be glorified in the Son. If in my name you ask me for anything, I will do it" (John 14:12-14).

Jesus' presence with the Father is a greater advantage for his disciples than his personal presence during his earthly ministry. Furthermore, this advantage extends to followers of Jesus Christ today. Jesus is able to intercede for us with the Father; and this is what he does! When we sin, he is our advocate with the Father, and his blood cleanses us from our sin. We have the assurance that we can bring *any* request before God. Jesus accompanies our prayers and assures us of an answer, which is consistent with the power and wisdom of God. Even when we are walking through life's deepest, darkest valleys we can find comfort and peace in the Lord Jesus, our good shepherd. Regardless of how hopeless any situation may seem, those who believe in Jesus have the promise of Jesus that their prayers to God do not fall on deaf ears. The one who trusts in Jesus possesses a promise from Jesus that provides security both for the future and also for the present.

Faith in God is not some magical key, which opens the secret lock to the door of a life of happy bliss, free from problems and difficulties. There will be moments in the life of the believer when he or she cannot see any way forward. There will be moments of sorrow and disappointment; feelings of loneliness and abandonment; times of weariness and weakness. There will be questions, which we in our limited human understanding will not be able to answer. There will even be questions about the value of faith. There were many, many things that Jesus' closest disciples did not understand during those final days of his life on earth, and there will be many things about Jesus that we do not understand—particularly when we are feeling at our lowest.

Jesus does not expect us to understand everything, nor is he upset with us for being confused in those moments when everything seems questionable. Rather, he simply asks us to trust God and to *trust him*. Believing in Jesus does not disappoint, for there is a promise of Jesus attached to this simple request. It is the dual promise of his abiding help in our present situation and of a future in his abiding presence!

14

Show Us the Father
John 14:8-17

SURELY JESUS was frustrated and disappointed when his disciples came to him with the request: "Show us the Father." It should not be too difficult for us to understand a little of his frustration and his disappointment when he was faced with this situation. For how do you portray someone who is not visibly accessible according to our normal categories of visual perception? Working with this text in John's gospel helped me when I was beginning to come to grips with the reality of my own father's death a few years ago. For a decade prior to his death the mental and emotional reality of my father's living presence in my life was not intimately bound up with his physical presence. We lived far apart from each other, he in the United States and I in Europe. We were far apart; and yet, in a sense he was present with me. Then suddenly, when he died, he was no longer with me in a physical sense, though the mental and emotional reality of his presence in my life was in many ways stronger than ever.

But if you asked me today to show you my father, how would I do this? I could show you a *photograph* of my father while he was still alive. But what would this really show you about my father? Visual images alone are very inadequate to communicate the reality of another person. How could Jesus show his disciples the Father? There was no photograph for him to produce from his pocket. He could not point them to some little statue, or image or shrine, and say: "Look, here is the Father!" or "This is what the Father looks like." Indeed, we know that God cannot be captured by our visual experience of reality. God the Father bursts the boundaries of our experiential knowledge. What we see and hear and touch and taste and smell cannot circumscribe God.

"Who has measured the waters in the hollow of his hand and marked off the heavens with a span, enclosed the dust of the earth in a measure, and weighed the mountains in scales and the hills in a balance?" asks the prophet Isaiah in rhetorical style. "Who has directed the spirit of the Lord, or as his counselor has instructed him? Whom did he consult for his enlightenment, and who taught him the path of justice? Who taught him knowledge and showed him the way of understanding? Even the nations are like a drop from a bucket, and are accounted as dust on the scales; see, he takes up the isles like fine dust. . . . All the nations are as nothing before him" (Isaiah 40:12-17).

How can we show someone a God like this? How can we approach a God who is immortal and who lives in unapproachable light? How can we portray a God whom no one has seen or can see (1 Timothy 6:16)?

"Lord, show us the Father," said Philip, "and we will be satisfied."

I think I can understand that Jesus might have been a bit frustrated when presented with this request. I think I can also understand, in a small way, some of his disappointment at this request. Jesus had been among his dis-

ciples for three years as the Son of God. They were aware
of the uniqueness of his person. They were aware of the
magnificence of his calling and of his ministry. They were
the first to recognize that he was the Son of the Father.

How then did they miss the point that in the person
and work of Jesus they were seeing the Father very clearly
portrayed before their eyes? "Whoever has seen me has
seen the Father," Jesus assured his disciples. There is truth
in the old proverb: "like father, like son." For better or for
worse, whether we want to admit it or not, it is true that
children tend to portray the image of their parents.

The British Broadcasting Corporation (BBC) produces a television program entitled "Small Talk," in which
children are asked a variety of questions and grownups
compete to predict how they will answer. In one particular broadcast someone had to predict how a certain little
boy would respond when asked if he would like to have a
girlfriend. After giving the matter some thought, the lad
replied that someday he would need someone to wash his
clothes, to cook his meals, and to clean up after him; so
yes, he would like to have a girlfriend! Now where, pray tell,
did a little boy of six or seven years come up with an idea
like that? Children can come up with a lot of novel ideas,
and it is interesting to see how often their ideas have been
influenced by things which were said or done by their parents at home!

The times are not few when driving in the car that
I have reminded my wife that her over-helpfulness as a
back-seat driver is very much reminiscent of a similar trait
in her mother. Neither are the times few when she has
had to remind me that some stupid joke I thought up or
some belligerent attitude I demonstrated was reminiscent
of similar traits in my father.

Jesus tells us: "If you have seen me, you have seen the Father. How can you say show us the Father?" God is best portrayed before our eyes by what God does. "Listen to the words which I speak," says Jesus, "these are the words of the Father. Look at the work I am doing; this is God's work. Look at the miracles which are happening around you; only God can do these kinds of things."

"Go tell John the Baptist what you see and hear," Jesus said on another occasion to John's own disciples. "The blind see, the lame walk, those who have leprosy are cured, the deaf hear, the dead are raised, the good news is preached to the poor" (see Matthew 11:2-6).

This is what God looks like. If you have seen the Son, you have seen the Father. God is seen in the things that God does. People cannot see someone who is invisible. People cannot approach unapproachable light. People cannot measure immeasurable infinity. People cannot think unthinkable thoughts. But people can see love in action. People will take notice when the blind, lame and deaf are healed and when the poor are receiving good news. If you have seen Jesus, you have seen God. If you have seen the Son you have seen the Father; the Father is seen by the things that the Father does.

Jesus does not leave the matter here, however. He carries the challenge one step further when he says to his disciples: "The one who *believes in me* will also do the works that I do and, in fact, will do greater works than these, because I am going to the Father. . . . I will ask the Father, and He will give you another Advocate to be with you forever. This is the Spirit of truth" (John 14:12, 16-17). It is not enough for Jesus' followers to look to him in order to see the Father. The world turns to the Church of Christ today, in the same way that Philip turned to

Jesus, with the request, "Show us the Father, and we will be satisfied."

How will we do this? How will we enable others to see the one who is unseen and who cannot be seen? How will we enable others to approach the God who is unapproachable light? How will we show people the Father? If someone asked me today to show him/her my father, who is no longer to be found in this world, I would not produce a photograph of his former likeness. Rather, I would display a pair of old, leather gloves that I keep in my garden shed. My father was a farmer. He gave those work gloves to me as a gift soon after his terminal illness had set in and he was beginning to think about giving gifts to his children. Some people might think this a silly gift, but it is one that I treasure! I never put on these particular gloves without thinking about my Dad. Whenever I put them on, I use them to do the same kinds of things my Dad would do, such as working in the garden, digging in the earth, planting seeds, pruning bushes. Though my father never wore these gloves himself, he might well have. For they are well worn. They have known some hard work, the kind of work that produces blisters and calluses and sore muscles in many parts of the body. The gloves are frayed around the edges and have a few holes in them. They are just like my Dad's gloves. If you could look at those old work gloves you would clearly see something of my Father.

Anyone who has seen Jesus has seen the Father because the works of the Son are the works of the Father. Anyone who believes in Jesus will do what Jesus has been doing. If you love me, he said, you will obey what I command. I will ask the Father and he will give you . . . a pair of work gloves . . . so that you can do the same work that God is doing. This is what it means to believe in Jesus.

The world looks to us today and says, "Show us the Father, and that will be enough. Show us the love of God in action in the world today, and we will be satisfied." Faith in Jesus Christ calls us to put on our God-given work gloves and rise to the challenge!

15

God is a Farmer
John 15:1-8

I MAKE NO excuses or pretenses when I refer to my father as a farmer. In some cultures agricultural enterprise is held in high esteem; in other cultural settings to call someone a farmer is almost an insult. When I call my father a farmer, however, I intend neither to praise him nor to insult him. My father truly was a farmer. This was his occupation. He was a tiller of the soil.

As the son of a farmer and as one who grew up on a farm, I can tell you many things about a farmer. I can tell you what fills a farmer's heart with joy; I can tell you what makes a farmer proud; I can tell you what it is that makes a farmer feel successful and honored.

But, of course, this is common knowledge, is it not? Everyone knows that it is the *harvest* that fills the farmer's heart with joy. It is the fruit of his or her labor that gives the farmer pride and honor and a feeling of success. This is particularly true if the harvest is a plentiful one. For the farmer, it is not just a matter of gathering in a harvest from the fields. Rather, farmers want to bring in a big, bountiful harvest. They are honored when the harvest, the fruit of their labors, is particularly successful, particularly plentiful.

Indeed, this is all fairly simple and straightforward. Who needs this sort of brilliant, enlightening commentary from some clever farmer's son in order to come up with these answers? However, I would suggest that there is much more than the bountiful harvest which gladdens a farmer's heart. Of course, the harvest is the climax of the growing season; it is indeed a joyous, glorious thing. But it is not the only glorious thing about farming. How many people would realize, for example, what a glorious thing a newly ploughed field is in the autumn? The whole year long, the soil of that field has served the farmer; it has received the seeds that were sown and has brought forth a harvest. Then in the autumn the farmer, in turn, serves the soil of that field by plowing it up. This is a glorious thing!

Who could imagine how proud a farmer can be in the springtime when all of the seeds he or she planted sprout up to form straight, even rows up and down the field? The proud farmer goes out regularly to inspect this miracle of nature. Farmers like to compare their growing crops with those of their neighbors. They are very proud if they can conclude that their fields look better than anyone else's.

Farmers are full of pride when their fields are 'pure'; that is, when they are free from weeds and clutter. A clean field of corn or soybeans is a glorious thing and well worth boasting about. A farmer (and the farmer's children!) might spend long days in the hot sun, walking up and down rows of soybeans to dig out the weeds by hand!

Farmers rejoice and are very proud when the crops in their fields are healthy and vigorous—when the plants are growing strong and hearty. When these plants prove their ability to withstand bad weather, damaging insects and nagging weeds, it is a good reflection upon the farmer who planted them. When the plants hold up in spite of drought or downpour of rain, and when they continue to grow and produce fruit in spite of the odds, this says something good about the one who oversees the field. This is truly a wonderful, glorious, joyous and praiseworthy thing. It is an honor for the farmer when the seeds that were planted grow and stand fast and produce fruit. I know all this because I have experienced it personally: *My father is a farmer!*

God is a farmer. This is what his son Jesus tells us about him in John 15:1. Jesus says: "I am the true vine and my father is the vine-grower—the *farmer.*" Of course, Jesus is using a parable here, when he calls his father a farmer. But this is not the first time in the Bible that God is depicted as a farmer, in particular as a vine-grower. This parable is prominent in the Old Testament, which portrays God as the vine-grower and the people of Israel as a grapevine planted by God himself.

"Let me sing for my beloved my love-song concerning his vineyard," writes the prophet Isaiah (see Isaiah 5). "My beloved had a vineyard on a very fertile hill. He dug it and cleared it of stones, and planted it with choice vines. He built a watch-tower in the midst of it, and hewed out a wine vat in it; he expected it to yield grapes, but it yielded wild grapes."

Again in Jeremiah 2:21, God speaks to his people: "Yet I planted you as a choice vine from the purest stock. How then did you turn degenerate and become a wild vine?"

This is precisely the same way that God is pictured in our text in John, as the conscientious, responsible, loving farmer, who plants in his vineyard only a choice, hybrid grape vine. He does not bother to plant a wild, spindly vine that will yield no fruit. This is precisely what Jesus is referring to when he claims to be the true vine. The true vine is none other than the choice, hybrid grapevine that produces only good fruit.

God is portrayed as the responsible farmer who takes care that his vineyard is in good order. He prunes away the unfruitful branches so that the vine will produce more and better fruit. Even the fruit-bearing branches are trimmed and pruned so that they may bring forth more and more fruit. God is the farmer whose highest concern is that the fruit-bearing branches remain firmly attached to the vine and that they withstand adverse weather and adverse conditions. God is the vine-grower who rejoices and who himself is honored and glorified when the vine and the branches produce abundant fruit. *God is a farmer.*

But this is not the only thing this parable about the vine and the branches teaches us. Jesus, for instance, is the choice, hybrid vine. In direct contrast to other potential vines, Jesus only produces good fruit. In fact, good fruit is the only kind of fruit, which Jesus can produce. There is no possibility of bad fruit coming forth from this vine. Bad fruit is an antithesis for this grapevine. If there is anyone who maintains that he or she belongs to Jesus Christ, the true vine, and that person produces inappropriate, unacceptable fruit, then we may be assured that this bad fruit stems from some other source. Bad fruit emerges from some other relationship, from some other root, than from Jesus Christ, who is the true vine of God.

On the other hand, anyone who fixes himself or herself to Jesus Christ and remains firmly attached to the true vine, that person will inevitably produce good fruit. There is no other possibility. This is the third insight we find in the parable of the true vine. God is the farmer, the vinedresser; Jesus is the choice, hybrid vine; and *you are the fruit-bearing branches* (see John 15:5).

The 'you' in this passage is naturally referring to Jesus' disciples. This includes all who belong to him and who have attached themselves to him. We who believe in Jesus are the fruit-bearing branches in the vineyard of God. God has already pruned us and made us 'pure' in as much as God has revealed his word and his will to us in Jesus Christ. Through this pruning and cleansing God increases our ability to bear fruit for him.

But bearing fruit is not something which branches, no matter how strong and healthy, can accomplish on their own. It is very significant that the word 'remain' ('abide' in some other English versions) appears seven times in only four verses in this parable. Only the branch that *remains* firmly attached to the vine will be able to produce fruit. In the same way, only the disciple who *remains* in Jesus will bear fruit. Whoever *remains* in Jesus will not simply bear fruit; but that person will produce *much fruit*. Whoever does not *remain* in Christ is like a branch that is thrown away and withers; those branches are picked up, thrown into the fire and burned. But whoever *remains* in Christ, and allows Christ's words to *remain* in him or her (for this *remaining* is a reciprocal relationship between a person and Christ), that person will ask whatever he or she wishes and it will be granted.

Is this not a most remarkable promise? "Ask for whatever you wish, and it will be done for you!" Oh, but this promise can hardly be understood and appreciated by someone who does not remain in Christ. The person who is outside of Christ hears this promise and prays in scorn: "Oh Lord, won't you buy me a Mercedes Benz!" That person asks for whatever he or she wants, and then expects, on the basis of the promise, that God will come through with the goods.

But there is an important prerequisite for the asking, for the wishing and desiring and for the receiving, which Jesus mentions in this promise. That prerequisite is summed up in the one word, *'remaining.'* "If you remain in me and my words remain in you, then you will ask whatever you desire and it will be given you." Believing in Jesus is a matter of remaining firmly and steadfastly rooted in Jesus.

Our steadfast remaining in Christ and his words remaining in us will determine both what we desire and what we ask for. Let us return for a moment to the parable. Consider a branch that is firmly attached to a healthy grapevine. What would it wish for? What would it desire? What would that branch ask for, if indeed a branch could ask for anything? What would be the goal of a branch that is continually being fed and nourished by the life-giving, fruit producing sap of a choice, hybrid grapevine? Would that branch request the ability to bring forth tiny, wild, sour grapes? Would it desire to produce apples, or olives, or tomatoes, or perhaps no fruit at all? Would that branch desire to remain short and small, with as few leaves and as few blooms as possible so that it would not have to work too hard or so that it would not come into close contact with other branches on the same vine?

Absolutely not! Anyone who has ever observed branches on a healthy grapevine knows precisely what those branches desire. They want to *grow*. They want to shoot forth and grow to be as long as they possibly can be. They want to produce as many leaves and blossoms as they can. Even when cut back and pruned, they still try to put on more foliage and more blossoms. They want to vine and wind around and join with other fruit-bearing branches to create a thick blanket of rich green foliage. They want to drink up every drop of sap they can draw from the vine in order to produce all the fruit they possibly can.

This is what the branches strive toward, when they remain in the vine! In fact, they wish and desire for nothing other than what the vine and the vine-grower wish and desire. It would not occur to them to desire anything else.

In the same way, if we remain in Christ and His words remain in us, we can ask for whatever we desire and it will be given to us. Our wishes and our requests will be at one with the wishes of the vine, who is Christ; they will be in harmony with the desires of the vine-grower, who is God. In other words, we will desire to grow and we will request the ability to produce fruit; and our request will be granted. We *will* grow; we *will* produce much fruit; for these results of growth and fruit bearing are not accomplished by us on our own. Rather they are accomplished through us, when we *remain* in Jesus Christ.

Here, then, is the beauty of the whole matter. Through our natural growth and bearing fruit, God is glorified and honored. God is honored when people who believe in Jesus receive what they desire and ask for; when they bear fruit; when they show themselves to be disciples of Christ by their steadfast abiding in Christ.

What is it, therefore, that causes the farmer to rejoice? In what does the farmer take great pride? What is it that brings honor and glory to the conscientious, responsible, loving farmer? Isaiah gives us the answer in no uncertain terms: "I will rejoice over Jerusalem and take delight in Israel" (Isaiah 65:19). God's own people—pruned, trimmed, purified and restored by him—are his delight and his joy and his pride.

God the farmer, the vine-grower is glorified when people believe in Jesus. God rejoices over his field, his vineyard! God rejoices when men and women come to him and join themselves to his choice, hybrid grapevine through faith in Jesus Christ. God is proud of those who withstand the adverse seasons and conditions and remain steadfast in their trust in Jesus. God is pleased with people who constantly and steadfastly are nourished and fed by his life-giving word. It makes God happy when men and women who are remaining in Jesus and in His word pray for growth and strive to bear fruit. It brings glory and honor to God, the vinedresser, whenever the branches of His choice vine produce much fruit.

Therefore, let us make God happy. Let us glorify Him by producing fruit. We can do it—but not by ourselves. We can only bring glory and honor, joy and pride to God, by remaining firmly fixed in Jesus Christ and His words in us!

16

Breathe on Me, Breath of God
John 20:19-23

B REATH IS life. Breath is spirit. Jesus breathed on his disciples with the words: "Receive the Holy Spirit" (John 20:20). This action and these words of Jesus occur in one of his appearances to the disciples following his resurrection from the dead. They recall the creative activity of God in Genesis 2:7 when God created Adam from the dust of the earth: "The Lord God formed man from the dust of the ground, and *breathed into his nostrils the breath of life;* and the man became a living being."

Actually, this is a very simple, logical piece of experiential wisdom. Whoever is breathing is alive; whoever stops breathing is dead. It is an awesome experience to sit at the deathbed of a friend or family member and to watch in those final moments. One breath is the boundary line between life and death! This is why mouth-to-mouth resuscitation is such an important part of any first-aid training. This is why the controversial artificial respirator machines have been developed and refined in the world of medicine. Whoever *breathes* is alive and whoever stops breathing dies. Breath is life!

In ancient oriental religious thought, breath is also 'spirit.' The Hebrew word which we translate as 'breath' in Genesis 2:7 is *ruach*. The same word is translated as 'spirit' or 'wind' in other Old Testament passages. This is also the case with the Greek word *pneuma*, which can mean 'spirit' or 'wind' or also 'breath' (particularly in the Greek translation of the Old Testament). As a matter of fact, the Genesis account of the creation of humankind is fairly explicit in its claim that breath is life *because* breath is spirit; it is the 'spirit-breath' of God!

There are other passages in the Old Testament, which play upon this close, inseparable relationship between breath and spirit, especially where human life and the Spirit of God are concerned. The creation account in Genesis 2 understands the spirit-breath of God to be the spark of human life in the nostrils of Adam. Later, in Genesis 6:3, the same relationship appears between God's Spirit and human life. This time, however, we see the relationship between life and spirit in the reverse sense of the creation account: "Then the Lord said, 'my spirit (*ruach*) shall not abide in mortals for ever, for they are flesh; their days shall be one hundred and twenty years.'" In other words, when God withdraws his spirit-breath from human beings, they die. The breath of God and the Spirit of God in this context are one and the same. This spirit-breath of God is absolutely essential for human existence. To be breathed on by God means to receive the indwelling, life-giving Spirit of God. In creation terms (especially *new* creation), this is precisely what it means to be called into life and into existence.

This is the very concept which provides the background for John 20:22 when Jesus breathes on his disciples and imparts to them the Holy Spirit. When people come into contact with Jesus and believe in him, Jesus breathes on them. That is, everyone who puts his or her trust in Jesus Christ receives from him the life-giving Holy Spirit of God. This is the meaning of the Pentecost event for Christians in every place and at every time throughout history. People who believe in Jesus receive his own creative, life-giving and life-sustaining Spirit-Breath!

Long before Jesus came in the flesh, the prophet Joel had proclaimed the advent of a day when the Lord would pour out his Spirit upon all people (see Joel 2:28-32). This would signal the ushering in of the last day and the new creation. It was a sign of the great salvation event that God was providing for a fallen world. The disciples of Jesus experienced the fulfillment of Joel's prophecy of the outpouring of God's Spirit when, after Jesus' ascension into heaven, they were gathered together in Jerusalem on the day of Pentecost. The place where they were gathered was filled with the sound of a rushing mighty 'wind' (the Greek word is *pneuma* — the same word for 'spirit'). The disciples were breathed on by Jesus; they were filled with the Holy Spirit and began to bear witness to Jesus Christ and the gospel. The Apostle Peter explained to the people who witnessed this event that God's promised life-giving Spirit was not limited to the men and women who comprised the original circle of Jesus' disciples. Rather, the promise is for all who repent and are baptized in the name of Jesus Christ. "The promise is for you, for your children, and for all who are far away, everyone whom the Lord our God calls to him" (Acts 2:39).

Everyone who believes in Jesus is breathed on by Jesus. But what exactly does it mean for Christians to be breathed on by Jesus and to receive his Holy Spirit? Actually, this means quite a number of things. The Spirit is the giver of life—*eternal life*. The Spirit provides comfort in the lives of Jesus followers. Jesus often referred to the Holy Spirit as the 'Comforter,' the *Paraclete*, the 'One who is called to stand beside' Christian believers in times of uncertainty and fear. The Spirit of God in our lives means also that we are children of God and that we have the privilege of calling out to God as 'Abba, Dear Father.' The Spirit of Truth is our teacher, the one who reminds us of Jesus' word and who leads us into all truth.

But in the specific context of John 20:19-23 the bestowal of the Holy Spirit has another very important meaning for the disciples of Jesus. The Spirit of God, which Jesus breathes upon those who believe in him, is implicitly bound together with a missionary task, with a missionary sending. "As the Father has sent me," Jesus said to his followers, "so I send you." When he said this he breathed on them and bestowed the Spirit of God, who would empower them for this missionary sending.

In this respect, when men and women receive the Holy Spirit of God in Christian baptism this has the very same significance as it had for Jesus at his own baptism when the Spirit of God descended upon him. Jesus' baptism signaled the beginning of his mission as the Lamb of God who would take away the sin of the world. His baptism was an act of commitment to God and to the calling of God. The pouring out of the Spirit was the empowerment he would require in carrying out his mission. Jesus clearly understood this to be the case. In his first recorded sermon in his hometown of Nazareth he preached from the text of Isaiah 61:1: "The Spirit of the Lord is upon me . . ." (see Luke 4:18ff). Jesus' message was this: "Today this scripture has been fulfilled in your hearing." The missionary sending which Jesus received in the outpouring of God's Spirit was a sending to bring people into God's presence, to share with them the good news of salvation, liberation and forgiveness of sins. It was a missionary task, which would culminate in suffering and sacrifice for the sake of others. (Suffering itself is another form of 'baptism' in which Jesus followers would also share.) As Jesus was preparing to leave his disciples and ascend into heaven, he breathed on them. He bestowed upon them the same Holy Spirit who had empowered his own ministry and said to his followers: "As the Father has sent me, so I send you."

The Holy Spirit is not simply a personal advantage for the individual Christian to possess and enjoy. The Holy Spirit is not only a Spirit of comfort and truth and knowledge, so that our personal and private lives are more fulfilled and happy. More than this, the Spirit of God is the motivating power of God who sends us to share good news with men and women who are in need of salvation, deliverance from oppression and forgiveness of sin. This same missionary emphasis is linked to the pouring out of the Holy Spirit on the day of Pentecost in the book of Acts. Prior to Jesus' ascension into heaven he instructed his disciples to wait in Jerusalem until they received the power of God through the outpouring of the Holy Spirit. This in turn was to be their signal that they would be Christ's witnesses in Jerusalem, in all Judea and Samaria, and to the ends of the earth (Acts 1:8).

The missionary sending which Christians have through the power of the Holy Spirit is an urgent missionary task. Only in Jesus Christ is there truly good news for the poor people of the world. Only through Jesus can the prisoners of this world be made free. Only in the name of Jesus do the blind people of the world receive their sight. Only in Jesus is the jubilee year of God's salvation a reality. Only in the name of Jesus Christ can the sins of men and women be forgiven. When Jesus empowered his disciples and sent them out, he told them, "If you forgive the sins of any, they are forgiven them; if you retain the sins of any, they are retained."

In this word of Jesus we find the extreme urgency of the mission for which Christians are empowered by the Spirit of God. Men and women, who live and die without Christ, live and die in bondage. Their hope for liberation from the oppression of sin lies in the faithfulness of Jesus' disciples in the world—the faithfulness of women and men, sons and daughters, old and young, servants and maids, who have been breathed on by Jesus Christ and have received his Holy Spirit. At the end of the day, believing in Jesus means participation in his own mission of salvation and redemption for a world in need of liberation.

17

Epilogue

FAITH LEADS to encounter with God, and encounter paves the way for faith. This is the testimony of the Fourth Gospel. Faith and encounter are not same thing; they are integral components, ongoing steps in the life of a Christian disciple. Believing in Jesus ushers the believer into new situations of engagement with God. Out of these encounters with God issues faith—renewed, deepened, and growing faith. Believing disciples follow Jesus to a marriage feast where they encounter in a fresh, unanticipated way his saving power. In the final analysis, the most important thing to be said about that particular occasion is that the disciples *believed in Jesus*. Believing Samaritans looking for the Messiah rush out to meet Jesus only on the word and witness of a sinful woman, and from this fresh encounter with God belief is born. So the story goes. Believing in Jesus leads to encounter with God, which, in turn, results in believing in Jesus.

Thus believing in Jesus is not simply the point of entry into a relationship with God, but part of the ongoing basis for that relationship. Believing in Jesus is the basis for ongoing access to a well of living water that never fails. Believing in Jesus opens the portals to an endless banquet feast where the bread from heaven never ceases. Believing in Jesus opens the way to a life of engagement with God; and this life does not end—not even when a believer dies! The ultimate encounter with God is the resurrection from the dead. This is an encounter of incredible, unimaginable proportion. It is an eternal encounter; and it is an encounter to which men and women only gain access through *believing in Jesus*.

I do not claim in this book to have exhausted the theme of *Believing in Jesus*, any more than John the Evangelist does. We have looked only at a few examples of what it meant in the lives of a few Christians to believe in Jesus. We have only considered a small number of countless encounters with God experienced by men and women who walked and talked with Jesus many years ago. If we were to attempt to record every encounter with God experienced by people down through the ages and to describe how those encounters with God arose from and led to faith in Jesus, "I suppose that the world itself could not contain the books that would be written" (John 21:25). Believing in Jesus is not a status, which we may attempt to define. It is rather a process in which we participate—a process of living, of new life. We call this process discipleship. Each day brings new encounter. Each day brings new challenge. Each day brings new understandings and new expressions of faith, as we drink from the well of living water and follow Jesus along the road of eternal life with God.

Select Bibliography

Brown, Raymond E. *The Community of the Beloved Disciple.* New York: Paulist, 1979.

Countryman, L. William. *The Mystical Way in the Fourth Gospel: Crossing over into God.* Philadelphia: Fortress, 1987.

Culpepper, R. Alan. *John, the Son of Zebedee: The Life of a Legend.* Personalities of the New Testament. Minneapolis: Fortress, 2000.

——. *The Gospel and Letters of John.* Interpreting Biblical Texts. Nashville: Abingdon, 1998.

Fortna, Robert, and Tom Thatcher, editors. *Jesus in Johannine Tradition.* Louisville: Westminster John Knox, 2001.

Kelly, Anthony J., and Francis J. Moloney. *Experiencing God in the Gospel of John.* New York: Paulist, 2003.

Koestenberger, Andreas. *Encountering John: The Gospel in Historical, Literary and Theological Perspective.* Grand Rapids: Baker, 1999.

Koester, Craig R. *Symbolism in the Fourth Gospel: Meaning, Mystery, Community.* 2d ed. Minneapolis: Fortress, 2003.

Kysar, Robert. *John's Story of Jesus.* Philadelphia: Fortress, 1984.

——. *Preaching John.* Fortress Resources for Preaching. Minneapolis: Fortress, 2002.

Lindsay, Dennis R. *Josephus and Faith: Pistis and Pisteuein as Faith Terminology in the Writings of Flavius Josephus and in the New Testament.* Arbeiten zur Geschichte des antiken Judentums und des Urchristentums 19. Leiden: Brill, 1993.

——. "What is Truth? An Enquiry into *Aletheia* in John 18:37-38," *Restoration Quarterly*, Volume 35 (1993) 129–145.

Painter, John. *The Quest for the Messiah: The History, Literature, and Theology of the Johannine Community.* Nashville: Abingdon, 1993.

Rensberger, David. *Johannine Faith and Liberating Community.* Philadelphia: Westminster, 1988.

Sloyan, Gerard S. *John.* Interpretation: A Bible Commentary for Teaching and Preaching. Louisville: Westminster John Knox, 1988.

Smith, D. Moody. *Interpreting the Gospels for Preaching.* Philadelphia: Fortress, 1980.

———. *John.* 2d ed. Proclamation Commentaries. Philadelphia: Fortress, 1986.

Thompson, Marianne Meye. *The Humanity of Jesus in the Fourth Gospel.* Philadelphia: Fortress, 1988.

Westermann, Claus. *The Gospel of John in the Light of the Old Testament.* Translated by Siegfried S. Schatzmann. Peabody, Mass.: Hendrickson, 1998.